DEFINING ACTS:
AGING AS DRAMA

Robert Kastenbaum

Jon Hendricks, Editor
SOCIETY AND AGING SERIES

Baywood Publishing Company, Inc.
Amityville, New York

Library of Congress Catalog Number 93-30310
ISBN: 0-89503-118-3 (Paper)
ISBN: 0-89503-119-1 (Cloth)

Library of Congress Cataloging-in-Publication Data

Kastenbaum, Robert.
   Defining acts : aging as drama / Robert Kastenbaum.
      p.   cm. - - (Society and aging series)
   Includes bibliographical references.
   ISBN 0-89503-119-1 — ISBN 0-89503-118-3 (pbk.)
   1. Aging- -Drama.   2. Aged- -Drama.   I. Title.   II. Series.
PS3561.A6999D44 1994
812'.54- -dc20   93-30310
                                                          CIP

Table of Contents

Foreword

A skyscraper under construction is an amazing sight. Its steel skeleton soars hundreds of feet into the air, festooned with pipes, cables, and concrete slabs. But the building must be furnished—carpeting installed, chairs put in, and family photographs set out—before the edifice comes to life. Modern science is the same. Its girders are made from statistics and controlled experiments, mathematics and mass surveys. But it, too, remains lifeless and empty, until it is furnished—with feelings, images, and personal experiences. Only then does knowledge become habitable, human—and alive.

This is what Robert Kastenbaum's plays do: they breathe life into our understanding of aging. The dramas in this collection are witty, provocative, ingenious, enigmatic, and haunting. But above all, they are alive. They move and speak, and what they say is eminently worth hearing.

The plays draw on Kastenbaum's many years of research in gerontology. Uniting the latest scientific findings with the ancient medium of drama, Kastenbaum explores the human face of aging. He uses magical images and dialogue to bring home the pain and promise of growing old, making statistical research sing and giving flesh to abstract policy debates.

In writing these plays, Kastenbaum joins two great streams of Western thought, what has been popularly called "left-" and "right-brained" thinking. Nineteenth century German philosophers christened these two modes of understanding, *Erklaren* and *Verstehen,* and Gisela Labouvie-Vief has more recently labelled them, *logos* and *mythos.* Modern science exemplifies logos, with a reliance on logic, mathematics and concrete evidence. Mythos, on the other hand, deals with images, feelings, intuitions—the substance of literature, myth, and fairy tales. Only the union of *mythos* and *logos, Verstehen* and *Erklaren*, provides true understanding, and that is the goal of Kastenbaum's dramas.

Gerontologists—and any aging adult—will easily recognize the fundamental issues that lie at the heart of these plays. "A Month of Sundays" tackles death; "The Girl in the Raindrop" addresses tragedy; "Father Muncrief's List" wrestles with meaning in life; "The Storyteller" and "Bedtime Story" confront intergenerational problems; "Why Does the Fireman?" explores the loss of roles and identity; "Activities of Daily Life" confronts dementia and disability. Yet the plays are not simply for scholars of aging. The dramas address timeless human issues. This is not surprising. After all, everyone who enters midlife becomes a student of aging, willingly or not. And today, as more and more people survive into old age, the issues loom larger. Kastenbaum's plays wrestle with problems most of us will eventually confront.

The topics are also the stuff of classical literature. "The Storyteller" or "Bedtime Story" recalls "Oedipus Rex," with its focus on tragedy and the rivalry between generations. "The Girl in the Raindrop" updates the Book of Job, and wrestles with the ancient problem of human suffering. Meanwhile, "Why Does the Fireman?" and "Activities of Daily Life" grapple with the same specter of madness in old age as does Shakespeare's "King Lear." If the themes of Kastenbaum's plays are timeless, it is because they deal with the substance of myth and fairy tales, with the fundamentals of human experience. Indeed, Kastenbaum's plays have much in common with myth and fairy tales. His dramas are magic, and take us into amazing worlds, where we discover unexpected meaning in everyday experiences of aging.

Yet Kastenbaum does not use familiar fairy tale themes—he reverses them with great effect. "Bedtime Story," for instance, is told from the viewpoint of the old woman, who would ordinarily be the witch in a story like "Hansel and Gretel." In inverting the usual focus of fairy tales, Kastenbaum forces us to reflect on issues in the plays. "Bedtime Story," I might add, anticipated by several years Stephen Sondheim's popular musical, "Into the Woods." Based on familiar fairy tales, Sondheim's production also shifts its perspective from that of youth to older adults. The parallel between Sondheim's musical and Kastenbaum's plays is not accidental. Many other writers, myself included, have turned to fairy tales and myths for insight about modern life. Surrounded by steel and science, we need moonbeams, stardust and fairy magic to remind us of the other side of human experience, of inarticulate feelings, fleeting intuitions, and poignant images—the language of the heart and soul.

If the plays in this book are magical, Kastenbaum does not employ traditional storytelling techniques. In fairy tales, the plot begins at the beginning and ends at the end, proceeding in roughly chronological order. Kastenbaum's plays follow a far more complex path. The dramas shift between perspectives, and leap back and forth in time. They comment on themselves, and ask the audience to intervene. They are really a series of evocative vignettes and interwoven motifs, rather than a traditional plot. Here the dramas are faithful to modern life and to a pluralistic, post-modern society. There is no single story or plot that gives meaning to our lives today, buffeted as we are by competing ideologies, pulled to-and-fro by conflicting roles, and disoriented by colliding cultures. Basic values and social conventions change constantly, accelerated by technological advances. The old drama of the hero, going off on a great quest and battling a well-known enemy, is too simple for our day. Yet what remains true now, as it was yesterday and the day before, is the human search for meaning, the need for reflection and consciousness. These are the basic motifs of Kastenbaum's plays, the underlying "plot," the story behind the stories.

Because of their shared themes, I recommend that the plays be read together. Although each can stand on its own, and most of them have already been performed that way, the dramas intertwine with each other, and gradually weave a magical tapestry. The cumulative effect is moving and evocative. Kastenbaum adds helpful and witty comments after each play, important for producing the dramas, but the plays themselves require no explanation. They speak eloquently.

Kastenbaum told me that he wrote these plays over a period of many years. He has long had an interest in literature, but found little free time for the Muses early in his scientific career. So he was forced to postpone his creative inspirations. His plight is universal, and anyone worried about paying the mortgage, sending children to college, closing deals, or writing grant applications, will understand. The Muses must wait! Yet there is a certain logic and poetic necessity in such a delay. Years of life experience bring depth and breadth to a writer's work, as these plays demonstrate.

In writing the dramas, Kastenbaum follows in the footsteps of scholars like Alfred North Whitehead and Jacques Monod—scientists who made their mark in youth with rigorous scientific work, and then turned in maturity to philosophy and the humanities. After advancing the cause of science, these writers discover its limits and reach for a more encompassing approach. The move takes courage—peers in the scientific community invariably raise their eyebrows at colleagues who write plays or read poetry in public. But the shift is essential, and the lesson is a necessary one for science and modern society in general. High technology and quantitative findings can only provide a skeleton upon which to build a culture. The substance must come from literature, myth, and fairy tales. In combining spirit and science, Kastenbaum and his plays blaze a trail others will hopefully follow.

Allan B. Chinen, M.D.
In the Ever After: Folk Tales of the Second Half of Life
Once Upon a Midlife

I. PROLOGUE

Drama in Aging and Aging in Drama

"Aging" suggests a slow, nearly imperceptible process. One thinks perhaps of erosion leisurely working its changes upon earth and stone. Viewed within long-term perspective, the changes may be dramatic, but the process itself has been as prosaic as water trickling downhill. Is it the same with people?

- Mr. Loring listens attentively as a nurse describes the type of care his wife will be needing when she is discharged from the hospital. It will be up to him to serve as primary careprovider at home, a responsibility that would overwhelm many a spouse. There is no doubt, however, about Mr. Loring's commitment to this challenge as he asks the nurse to "Waltz me around one more time on the medications." The weight of his eighty seven years will not deter him from doing his utmost to care for the woman who has shared his life for more than sixty years.
- The old woman has more on her mind than dying. Mrs. Gillespie's three daughters have been rivals ever since childhood. Yes, they love each other deeply, but there is also a strong vein of competition and resentment that now threatens to break through the surface and do lasting harm to their relationships. The arena of contention will be the division of personal items from the rather impressive estate that Mrs. Gillespie and her late husband had built up over the years. Can she find a way to keep the deadly politeness of her three adult daughters

3

from erupting into painful confrontations and recriminations? Can she somehow prevent this deterioration of relationships and foster a farewelling process that leaves them all with a sense of warmth and support?

- It happened again this morning. Twice. Mr. Phillips could not think of the names of two of his regular clients. This was not like him at all. Was forgetting now a pattern? How much worse would it become? Could he go on as a confident and respected professional, or would he have to give in to this insidious process—and would others some day soon be referring to him as an "Alzheimer"? Would, in fact, the day come when his own name and identity were beyond reach? In the meantime: how would he just get through today?

AGING AS ENHANCED DRAMA

Life is drama at every moment (well, sometimes it is comedy, too). Both vigorous and fragile, life is ever at peril from the same environment that provides its sustenance and venue. At the human level the drama of life is heightened by self awareness, along with the propensity to spin out webs of meaning and fantasy in which we entrap both each other and ourselves. Other creatures also take nourishment, mate, deal with their offspring, and shuffle off this mortal coil. But we seem to be the only ones who worry about cholesterol level, sexual morality, childrearing competence, and living wills. We also seem to be the only ones who are in conflict with our own nature. It is our race and no other that envisions altruism, piety, truth, beauty, and transcendence only to behave so often in cruel, heedless, hypocritical, tawdry, and solipsist ways that surpass the imaginings of our fellow creatures.

Growing and being "old" heightens the drama. We know that the prologue and first act have long since been played. Significant characters in our scenario have already exited. Do we still have the time, opportunity, and spirit to fulfill our most cherished goals? Can we hold on to the tokens of love and residues of triumph that time has given to us when time itself increasingly threatens to take them all back? How long can we still be who we are? And who are we yet to become? Furthermore, when that final curtain is ready to fall, how will we play out the scene? And how, if at all, will the world be changed by the fact that we once lived and now have died?

There is something inherently dramatic in even the ordinary moments. Will we give in to temptations to withdraw from social contact, leave decision-making to others, and slip into a cocoon of isolation and idiosyncratic routine? Will we organize ourselves around the proposition that tomorrow should be a replica of today—if not yesterday? Or will we bristle at every touch of age's hand and concede nothing to time and expectation? Most of us have—or will—experience the claims of both tendencies. We may think of these polar attractions as the psychomagnetic forces of past and future that operate on us while themselves being influenced by "gravity's rainbow." Should we (can we?) go forward? Should we (can we?) go back? Or should we (must we?) root ourselves into a present blind moment until eventually it opens beneath us and ejects us into the void?

Past, present, and future meld into new and unique relationships as our lives compress in time. The drama is in our dawning, yet incomplete awareness of change. The drama is in our avoiding, our facing, our choosing. The drama is in rediscovering or reinventing ourselves to stake everything between one tick of the clock and the next.

And so, Mr. Loring takes responsibility for home care of his frail and vulnerable wife. Mrs. Gillespie sets aside her own doubts and commits herself to bringing those tense and distrustful daughters into harmony before she leaves them forever. Mr. Phillips faces an immediate decision: should he meet the next client with confidence, or pack it in? But he also is starting, for the first time, to see himself within the context of his whole life instead of merely charging ahead to "earn brownie points" that have never quite added up to self-fulfillment.

Aging is an exercise in enhanced drama: basic conflicts escape the restraints we have imposed on them and assert themselves for resolution without further delay. Both reality and value demand their due. Whether or not we are prepared for our parts, time will no longer wait for us. We must act.

Unlike the process of erosion, aging is life itself as it operates through experienced time between as well as within people. As such, it is universal drama, but also drama that is unique to this time, this place, this person.

RESTORING DRAMA TO GERONTOLOGY

The natural drama in aging has been overshadowed to some extent by research and policy agendas. *Methods and procedures. Quantitative analyses. Highly focused objectives. Measurable outcomes. Cost effective-ness. Objectivity.* These are among the dominant "stage directions" in research and policy approaches to human aging. And yet the dramaturgical spirit can be discerned behind the masks of disinterested objectivist and social technician.

A derivative of eighteenth-century Rationalism, today's research and policy enterprises also are marked by the ritualistic theatricalism that contributed not a little to that movement's success. (Comte, the father of operationalism, was also one of the most gifted ritual-makers of his time.) Research and policy endeavors are among the most highly scripted of human activities and must conform to the exacting demands of their critics and audiences. Woe to the researcher or policy-maker who departs from the assigned role and thereby breaks the spell. The theater of geron-tological science and policy-making, like any compelling theater, requires the suspension of disbelief. At least for the moment, we must not seem to notice the omissions and inconsistencies. All these multivariate multi-points-of-measurement statistics and all these cost-benefit projections should keep us sufficiently bedazzled to inhibit rude questions such as: "But where are the people? Where are the situations? *What is at stake?*"

To be sure, drama also has its experimental and policy dimensions, but our concern here is with the extent to which gerontology has developed a kind of anti-theater theater. By this I mean a selective representation of the human landscape without the spirit, longings, risks, conflicts, tragedies, and triumphs that one finds in real life and its distillation in the dramatic and literary arts.

This is not a critique of gerontological research or policy making as such. I read and on occasion contribute to these literatures, but I just don't find Mr. Loring, Mrs. Gillespie, or Mr. Phillips there. I don't think I am the only one who finds it difficult to bridge the gap between the scholarly and professional literature on the one hand and the living reality of aging men and women on the other.

Perhaps this is why I have crossed the line now and then. Perhaps it is just for my own sense of aliveness and coherence that I have written the theater pieces offered in this book as well as a number of others that didn't seem to fit here. I also have the feeling, however, that these characters, along with their urgings and predicaments, are the ones who actually created the plays. They wanted out. They wanted to enact their "Most

Tragical Farces" for other minds than my own. They wanted the opportunity to flit in and out of classrooms, conferences, and other venues where the gerontologically-inclined gather to inform, inspire, or depress each other. They even wanted the opportunity to ambush on occasion those who seldom reflect on time's way with us.

ON THE DANGERS OF DRAMA

But, then, perhaps we should leave gerontology as it is: an earnest field of inquiry and practice that has challenges enough by virtue of its complex subject matter, unfulfilled quest for a unifying paradigm, and continuing resistance from individuals, agencies, and institutions that would simply prefer to have old age and death go away. Restoring drama to gerontology is not likely to bear short-term benefits with respect to the challenges that have just been identified. In fact, it might well prove to be a destabilizing force. Opening the stage door just a crack could have such troubling consequences as:

- Reminding us that the human situation seldom lends itself to neat and definitive resolutions;
- Questioning the relationship between the observer and the observed, as well as among "reality," "fantasy," "illusion," and "construction";
- Recruiting inner doubts, anxieties, hopes, and ideals that we may have thought had been safely locked away from our scholarly and professional selves;
- Revealing the ambiguities and contradictions that mark our encounters with the aging of ourselves and others;
- Energizing anew our sense of expectations, possibilities, and alternative scenarios;
- Encouraging our own dramatic instincts—by far a more natural and holistic orientation than the recently cultivated and still brittle attitude of objectivity.

All in all, opening ourselves to the passions, demands, and ambiguities of drama would introduce a challenging alternative to contemporary gerontological science and policy-making. Drama is likely to escape quickly from an assigned role as simply one educational method among others: the purposes of our work and its relationship to our own lives may also be subject to revision if not transformation.

WHAT IS THIS BOOK AND WHAT
SHOULD WE MAKE OF IT?

This is a collection of mostly rather short plays written by a person who has been active for some years in the related fields of lifespan human development, aging, and thanatology. (I don't much care for the latter term, but it has no serious rivals; I think of thanatology as the study of life with death left in.)

First: what these plays are not. They are not dramatizations of standard gerontological issues, nor attempts to translate concepts into stage characters. They do not aspire to the lofty genre of soap opera, Monday night movie, or dinner theater, and make no attempt to pass as quasi-documentaries. Most of all, they are not simplistic and safe little moral lessons in theatrical guise.

Within its limited scope, each play is a set of encounters with what the human spirit encounters at the depths and edges of its experience. There is everywhere a kind of search or quest. However, this does not guarantee that our characters will grasp the torch of self-illumination when it finally comes to hand, or that "family values" will invariably triumph. Familiar stereotypes of the old person appear now and then, but seldom linger in the expected pose. A few of our characters want to be admired, some want to be understood, and most want to be loved. All want to become at one with your existence, if only as a small but insistent memory-thorn.

These plays can be effective in gerontological/thanatological education at both beginning and advanced levels, and with either "plain" or "fancy" presentation.

- As an assigned reading with follow-up discussion. In asking students to read a particular play, the instructor might pass along a few guiding questions. The assignment could include a brief paper as well as class discussion.
- As a script-in-hand class presentation. One set of students reads the play to the others, with follow-up discussion.
- As a stimulus to the students own empathy and imagination. The individual reading and/or class script-in-hand presentation can be followed by improvised variations. How else might Charlotte have

handled that situation? What would you do in Father Muncrief's place?

- A "worked up" script-in-hand presentation could be made as a special feature of meetings designed to interest others in gerontological/thanatological issues, or as part of disciplinary or interdisciplinary gerontological meetings. A follow-up panel discussion could relate this presentation to the aims of the meeting.
- A full production could be presented at a gerontological conference, or offered to the community in a cosponsored arrangement between a gerontology program and an educational or community theater company.
- A "for ears only" production could be presented on a cooperative basis with educational or local radio. (Several of the plays lend themselves particularly well to this type of treatment.)

Each play in this collection is followed by a brief "Notebook." These entries are intended to ease the way for instructors, directors, and others to develop their own plans for utilization. A typical "Notebook" touches on some of the play's characters and themes, its relevance to the literature and real world gerontology, and some thoughts about presentation. There are many ways in which educators might develop and integrate a particular play within their own needs and context.

In general, these plays do not require extensive production efforts. One does ask for fairly elaborate production and serious rehearsal time to make its optimal impact (*The Girl in the Raindrop*) although this one, too, can be presented effectively by talented readers.

I would suggest that readers take a few minutes with the following chapter in which the main characters from all the plays are briefly introduced. The plays can be read in any sequence, of course, but I would make the further suggestion that the "Notebooks" be ignored until one has completed the plays themselves.

A concluding chapter returns to themes touched upon here. It is suggested that both the aging person and the field of gerontology could benefit by exploring the dramatist's paradigm of situated action as an evocation and evaluation of lived experience.

The first of the plays to be given a public performance takes its title from a hoary vaudevillian straight line, "*Why Does the Fireman . . . ?*" The scene was a Toronto hotel, where I was to deliver the incoming presidential address for the American Psychological Association's Division on Adult

Development and Aging. I started off as though intent on fulfilling the audience's expectations with a rambling introduction, but then transformed myself into an old man before their very eyes, while the innocent-looking space around me converted itself into a stage area. The audience was provoked again when the loveliest woman in the audience suddenly rose from her seat and interrupted the proceedings with a "Knock-knock!" The eminent gerontologist sitting next to her whispered urgently, "Sit down, Bunny! What are you doing? You're ruining the play!" However, Bunny Kastenbaum was an integral part of the proceedings as she created a memorable Dr. Gerry.

One of my own lasting memories came after the play had run its course and the cast granted safe conduct by its generous audience. I had silvered my then-youthful locks as part of my getting-into-character bit and now I had the chance to inspect the results in the washroom mirror. "I'm going to wash that age right out of my hair," had been my intention. But I stayed my hand. For the rest of the evening I enjoyed the look of age. "Not bad," I thought, "a stranger might even think that a little wisdom goes with the silver hair!"

And now, and for some time now, the silver no longer washes out. I thank the protagonist of *Why Does the Fireman?* for having offered this opportunity to step into the role of aged person a bit ahead of time, and permit myself to hope that perhaps a little of the good stuff may have rubbed off. Perhaps somewhere in this collection you will also find a character or two that can be taken to heart. Like 'em or not, they're all anxious to meet you.

Meet The Characters

Welcome to the neighborhood. (Mr. Rogers had another appointment, sorry.) If you are curious about the characters you will be meeting, then you've come to the right place. No, I won't pre-tell their stories or give too much away. But there's nothing wrong with a little neighborly gossip, is there? Perhaps you will find this useful in identifying folk you particularly want to meet (or avoid). Since we only have a moment, we will have to limit ourselves to major characters. This means I will be in a lot of trouble with the rest of them, but that's my problem. We'll just take the characters as they come, or as you would meet them if you sauntered along from the first to the last play in this collection.

"Tell them I write only with the taste of fresh blood on my lips." Should we believe her? *The Storyteller* is a very-much-in-control woman who looks to be in her early 70's, but could also be much older. She may or may not comply with aspiring *Young Woman's* request to help her become a writer. "Somebody needs to keep the stories coming." Their interaction literally sets the stage for the compelling but uncertain endeavor of interweaving lives and stories in search of an elusive wholeness.

"Were you always so old and useless?

"Heavens, no! I was once young and useless. Useless didn't matter, then, because I was a sweet and lovely thing. *Old* and useless is something else!"

This *Old Woman* is remembered by history as a prototypical witch. We learn the truth (sure, we do!) in *Bedtime Story*. If *The Storyteller* is a terse black-and-white sketch, then *Bedtime Story* is the rambunctious, colorized, and, literally, larger-than-life big screen version. Her numerous companions in adventure include some of the most famous names in Storyland, although not always operating under the names known to history. A *Child* and *Young Mother* of our own day co-create this tale one evening, but the characters soon take the story into their own hands (and paws). *Bedtime Story* explores the dangerous terrain involved in getting from youth to age as well as from The Age of Magic to whatever the heck it is we have today. "In the middle of the woods you will probably meet a disgusting old witch who will eat you up and that will be that." Not for the faint-hearted, but for those willing to consider ancient and modern times within the same parable.

> "God took Mother
> Off to Heaven.
> But I'm still here
> And almost seven.
> I live in joy and never cry
> And God knows all the reasons why."

Charlotte and her half-brother *Nelson* (who she has a sort of half-Nelson on) are late Victorian children when we meet them, and very old people of our own time when we take our leave. We visit with them on various Sundays in their lives as each attempts to distill meaning from the particular mix of fantasy and reality available to their generation. Each has developed a characteristic way to keep from losing everything all the time but, in the meantime, what has happened to their lives? *Workman,* the gravedigger and more, cautions us all:

> "Listen, you can't go around believing
> Everything you hear, just because it is said
> By a man with sweat steaming down his face
> And one foot in the grave."

A Month of Sundays, with thanks to *Charlotte* and *Nelson,* might provide a life time's worth of sensitivity to what we speak of academically as "cohort effects."

> "Why does the urban, downwardly mobile chicken
> Cross the road?"
> "Suicidal, I suppose."
> "Why do old people commit suicide?"
> "To get to the other side."

This dislocated exchange takes place between *Old Man* and *Dr. Gerry,* the freshly coined gerontologist who is attempting to interview him for her book. It is an existential vaudeville in which an objectivist outsider and a highly subjective person rooted in his own long life attempt to establish the claims for their respective realities. Both come away with more and less than they had in mind. *Why Does the Fireman?*

"Because. . . . There is still fire some place.
Because there is still something left to burn.
Why does the fireman?
Because he must!"

The characters here also include *Waldo* who may be the ultimate old-person-treated-as-furniture, and *Madame Futura,* who may have found a way to evade negative age stereotypes, although it's an act difficult to sustain. Like many flesh-and-blood lives, the characters in *Why Does the Fireman?* may seem to have a difficult time of it when reduced to a plot summary—but moment by moment each contrives to be his/her own unrepentant self.

"Try calling to them—well, it's hopeless.
I've lost their names and they know it.
A memory like mine makes it hopeless."

Mr. Ah-Uhm may not even remember his own name, so how can we know it? In *Activities of Daily Life,* he is nominally participating in a reality orientation session. But what reality is he seeking, and what reality seeks him?

"What comes after
After the being talked at
After the being walked off from
After the door closes as doors close
in a dream
Soundlessly
After the empty room hears my apology . . ."

Perhaps it is just as well that our visit with *Mr. Ah-Uhm* is so brief. Another moment or two and we might begin to wonder about our own . . . (now, what was I going to say?).

"I see the confession in Old Mr. Wigby's tight grip on the leash of his ugly and unfortunate dog."

We are now with an elderly priest as he inspects Midvale from his privileged viewpoint in the belfry. *Father Muncrief* is about to make a list. Two lists, actually, "For" and "Against."

"Even unpleasant thoughts become more bearable
When they are made up into a list. . . .
Lists are real and manageable.
Even when nothing else is.
All right, then!"

In *Father Muncrief's List,* he not only wants to make the right decision, but to make this decision rightly, that is to say, in an orderly and rational way. Does he succeed?

"Father Muncrief? Who did you beget?
Who did you fashion from your loins and hers?
Who did you hold against the night?
Whose sweat did you taste?"

Mr. Ah-Uhm and *Father Muncrief* are not the only old men who attempt to find their way through reality, fantasy, hypocrisy, and menace.

"Dear Earth, Dear Mother:
Madam—I cannot explain why we rush
So swiftly into your dark embrace.
Yet, why roses these days exhale the
Stench of blood is not so difficult to explain.
I should not be surprised if tomorrow's roses
will have become carnivorous!
We are all killers, dear Madam."

It is the aged *Sigmund Freud* who is more troubled about the future of the self-destructive human race than his own intractable and agonizing illnesses. In *Vienna, City of My Dreams,* Freud does have a personal agenda to go along with his universalistic concern: the quest for his own ultimate identity and meaning.

> "Perhaps I must also speak with Father.
> But which Father?
> The old man who snored beside my mother
> and had so few words for me?
> Our Father Which Art Raging in an
> Old Testament whirlwind?
> Or enthroned in a New Testament paradise?
> My Fatherland who crushes his own children
> with iron jackboots?
> Or myself, a father-figure to some and a target
> to not a few?
> Father—where are you?"

We meet Freud at that historical moment when he is attempting to reply to a question from Albert Einstein on behalf of the League of Nations while the Nazis are systematically destroying all of the psychoanalytic movement they can get their hands on. He must review his own doubts and beliefs before he can respond to the public challenge.

> "Here I am and there I am. Me and me.
> Me down there and me up here.
> Look at that Down There Me!
> What a stupid little snot! She can't do a thing!
> . . . Do yourself a favor—get buried!"

Valerie is not having a near-death experience. She considers herself instead to be enduring a near-life experience. *The Girl in the Raindrop* is a thirteen-year-old with life-threatening leukemia who is restricted to a reverse-precautions isolation room.

> "So I make up a lot of stuff.
> I put some of it into this play. Hope you like it."

Her quest for comfort, understanding, and meaning makes things very uncomfortable for the adult establishment, including her physician, parents, *Bible Lady, Reality Man,* and even *The Big Guy. The Bikeman,* who we know under many other names, is her most attentive companion most of the way, but perhaps not an ideal companion in all respects. Even *Bible Lady* is a bit shaky:

> "God has to be tough with the wrong kind of
> People. But God's message is love, not leukemia.
> God's message is everlasting love, not death."
>
> *"So it's love when God gives kids leukemia?"*
>
> "God doesn't actually *give* kids leukemia."
>
> *"Well, He doesn't exactly not give kids
> Leukemia, either."*

The tough questions do not always wait until the later years of life, especially, as with *Valerie,* when now may be all that she has. Is she to be censured for seeking answers at more than one level? And does the adult world have anything to offer *The Girl in the Raindrop* other than its own confusion, discomfort, and secondary gains?

> "What are we supposed to learn from this—hah?
> Aren't we *supposed* to learn from this?
> Isn't dying OK and death and grief if we learn something
> from it? That's the buzz brother. Buzz, buzz!"

So that's the neighbors, some of them. Perhaps these characters include a few you would like to know better and introduce to your students, colleagues, and either Significant or Insignificant Others.

One more thing! There's a vacant place just down the street. Waiting for your characters, your story.

II. THE PLAYS

The Storyteller

The Storyteller is a woman in her early 70's. She is sparing in her expressive movements and slow, thoughtful, and deliberate in speech, but this outward demeanor is fueled by an intense and guarded inner life. In disclosing to the audience, her attitude is of one who is inclined to preserve her reserve and is judging the situation carefully before deciding whether to say anything more. In her garb and manner, *The Storyteller* is not easily assimilated to stereotypes of a particular geo-ethnic or socioeconomic class; there is something of a timeless and universal quality about her.

AT RISE: *THE STORYTELLER (ST) is seated on a stool, hands folded in her lap, head lowered in contemplation or slumber. She raises her head and inspects the audience at her own leisure, giving little clue as to her attitude.*

ST: You want to be a writer?
Write.
What more can I tell you?
What do they tell you?
Theories? Yes, of course, theories. Check lists? Exercises?
Reading how famous writers write. and now interviewing a famous writer yourself. For extra credit!
We are simply wasting each other's time. Go back to your theories and check lists. For extra-credit—tell them anything. Tell them I write only when the lunar phases correlate with my

numerological calculations. Tell them I write only with the taste of fresh blood on my lips. Tell them I write only when the rent comes due. Tell them anything. Not all liars can write, but all writers of accomplishment can certainly lie.

One serious question? Fine.

How do I get started with a story? Is that your problem, dear? The getting started? What I do may be helpful to you. I start by starting—and then waiting for the story to tell me how to proceed. Are you sure you want to hear this? All right, then. You start, say, with a person. That is all you have at the moment. This idea of a person.

Spot rises on YOUNG WOMAN (YW)

Good. Today this idea of a person wants to be a young woman. Like you. And so we have this young woman. Fine. Where is she? Where might she be?

YW walks about hesitantly for a moment, followed by spot.

In a room, I think. This young woman will be in a room. What should this room be? It must be some kind of room.

YW enters a new space schematically arranged as a bedroom with bed and vanity.

Yes. There is a young woman and she is in a bedroom. But precisely where is she in this bedroom and what is she doing?

YW's actions unfold in keeping with the narrative, sometimes a little ahead of the words

The young woman is sitting on the bed. I notice that she is wearing a business suit. Wearing a business suit and sitting on the bed. How is she sitting? Not comfortably. On edge. Literally on edge. Perhaps she is nervous. Why would the young woman in a business suit be nervous sitting on the edge of a bed?

	I don't know yet. But my curiosity has been aroused. I would like to know why she is there and what is making her nervous. Mostly, I would like to know—
YW:	What's going to happen next?
ST:	Precisely. Do you know? Neither do I. And so I wait for her to instruct me further. Oh, but that's it!
YW:	She's waiting!
ST:	So what do we have now?
YW:	An idea of a person who is a young woman who is wearing a business suit who is in a room that is a bedroom who is sitting on edge at the edge of the bed—waiting.
ST:	Who is she waiting for?
YW:	A man! [*Blushes*].
ST:	She is waiting for a man. But how do you know that? What does she *do* that reveals her mind?

YW is uncertain for a moment, then rises and crosses to the vanity. Looks at her reflection in the mirror, adjusts her hair, etc.

YW:	I—she—wonders if she looks—right. If she looks appealing . . . to a man.
ST:	How does she feel about the way she looks just now?
YW:	There's nothing actually wrong with the way she looks.
ST:	But how does she *feel?* Excited? Ready to burst into flame? Or into tears?

YW places hands over her face, holds back tears, turns away from the mirror

Light fades on bedroom scene. STORYTELLER rises, and takes a step forward.

ST:	There is a young woman. We do not know her name. She is in a bedroom. We do not know whose bedroom or where. She is wearing a business suit. We do not know why. She is waiting for a man. We do not know who he is—what will happen when he arrives—or if he will actually come. A story is telling itself in its own way and in its own good time.

STORYTELLER strolls to the darkened bedroom space. She gestures. Lights rise. YW is still there, holding a distraught pose, turned away from the mirror, a fist clenched in tension. STORYTELLER stands at the periphery of the space.

        I am the storyteller. But I am not the story. I have no reason, no right to intrude myself. I must keep the observer's distance. I must limit myself to the Storyteller's voice. I must not feel for her—too much. I must not judge her—too much. It is for my listeners or readers to feel, to judge, to engross.

YW: You're talking about me!

ST: Characters must also respect their limits.

YW: Is that all I am to you—a character?

ST: It is not easy at first. You want to be part of the story. The story wants to be part of you.

YW: I am part of you!

ST: She is becoming more lively, more interesting. Anger will do that.

YW rushes to the near edge of the bedroom space. They are now separated only by the symbolic border.

YW: You help me! You help me get through this! You were the one started it all.

ST: Now is that true? I think not.

YW: All right, I started it, too. But I need your help.

ST: My help with what?

YW: With what comes next. With getting through what comes next.

ST: What makes you think I can help?

YW: Because—because you're the famous author. You're the Storyteller. You're the—mean old bitch who doesn't have to be so mean if she didn't enjoy it!

ST: Well, when you put it that way. . . . Fine. Clear out. I'm coming in.

YW: What do you want me to do?

ST: You be me.

STORYTELLER enters the bedroom space confidently. YW exits this space hesitantly. YW will observe ST for a moment, and then, catching on, perch herself on ST's stool. ST meanwhile first takes up YW's former distraught pose, then abruptly breaks it, throwing back her head and laughing. She turns to face the mirror, leaning both hands on the vanity.

YW: Gosh, what's happening? I think we need some externalization of inner speech—thought balloons—or is that too melodramatic?

ST: [*To her mirror image*] You make me laugh! You make me sick! Foolish little girl! Foolish little girl in a business suit. Foolish little girl in a business suit waiting for—do you really suppose—a man?

YW: I think there should be footsteps at the door about now.

Footsteps are heard. STORYTELLER panics momentarily, then quickly recomposes herself, although not completely. She distances herself from the door as far as possible, moving to the other side of the bed.

ST: But it can't be him!

YW: Somebody is there. Somebody is standing on the other side of the door.

VOICE I: [*A mature man*] It could be me.

VOICE II: [*A young man*] Or me!

VOICE I: Make up your mind, will you?

YW: Somebody is there. OK. Somebody is standing there on the other side of the door. But who? Is it the man she has been expecting—or not expecting?

ST: [*Quietly*] Let this be the moment then.

YW: I like this. I like being the Storyteller.

VOICE I: Are you ready for me yet?

VOICE II: Or me?

YW: I like—well, I think best—that I continue. I make it through. Characters will laugh and suffer and exit. I will continue. I will make it through because somebody needs to. Somebody needs to keep the stories coming. Somebody needs to keep the stories going.

ST: Let this be the moment that ends all hope and all fantasy.

VOICE I: I am always approaching a door. Maybe the same door. It's almost like a dream.

VOICE II: Same here.

VOICE I: I am always somebody's plot element. Somebody's next. Somebody's footsteps at the door.

VOICE II: I'm not that good at waiting.

VOICE I: Then why don't you give the cue this time?

A knock is heard. STORYTELLER gathers her courage and slowly approaches the door. Just as she reaches the door she looks questioningly at YW who recognizes that she has a decision to make and does so. She gestures to STORYTELLER, and, by mutual understanding, they exchange places again. As they cross each other's paths:

YW: It's still my life. I'll take it from here.

ST: Didn't you enjoy playing the mean old bitch?

YW: Yes, I did. Great practice! But it's not my turn yet.

ST is now again perched on stool, hands in lap; YW has her hand on the doorknob

ST: You want to be a writer?
Write.
What more can I tell you?
Start with a person. Start with a person in a place at a moment. Start with a person not entirely different from yourself in a place not so different from this place at a moment very much like this moment.
Give your voice to this person at the instant life becomes story and story becomes life.
Grow old with your storied life.
Remain young with your storied life.
What more can I tell you?

YW opens the door part-way, then speaks with lively confidence

YW: So it is you! Let's get on with it!

YW walks through door to take the arm of her unseen visitor

NOTEBOOK

We have been told stories all our lives. Myth, religion, philosophy, history, poetry, drama, and education may all have had their origins in storytelling. Mostly, we accept these stories. Perhaps it is more accurate to say that these early-heard and often-repeated tales are absorbed into our bones and rehearsed by our viscera to the point where acceptance is not a relevant concept. And, mostly, we grow up around these primal stories, supplementing them with a few additional received tales.

We also grow old around these stories. Have I not become all the stories I have heard and read, as well as my experience's commentary on these stories? From childhood's hour I am Abraham, Joseph, and Isaac. I am the Selfish Giant and the Chinese Nightingale. I am The Kid from Tompkinsville in his rookie season—clackety-clack of spiked shoes in the dugout—and Zorro out-dualing The Bad Guy, even though Zorro is the one in black. I am the *I am* invented for me through the family narrative as well as the *we are* emerging from the family's continuing act of self-invention and revision.

The Storyteller gives us two women who dare to create their own stories and then to share together in an act of co-creation. Each takes a risk in sharing. Both youth and age relinquish something of their protective bubbles by opening to the other. Only through such risk, however, does the opportunity arise for age to bequeath and youth to receive. The process also flows in the other direction, does it not? Youth offers age a sense of affirmation and continuity by taking up the story (though, of course, on its own terms).

The Storyteller provides an invisible framework for all the other plays in this collection. It is here that the "workings" are most clearly exposed, as in a clock with a transparent lid. Human relationships, however, are notoriously more nuanced, conflicted, and unpredictable than clockwork. And so we detect ambivalence, role ambiguity, and an evolving sensitivity to alternative views of reality.

The presentation can be simplicity itself. *The Storyteller* is suitable for script-in-hand (but well rehearsed) performance. Two skillful readers and as many high stools are all that would be required. The effectiveness can be enhanced by switching off audience lighting and providing each reader with her own floor-standing lamp. It is not a bad idea to have the scripts encased in oversized black covers to emphasize rather than conceal the fact that this is to be a reading. The script-in-hand technique can also be used in productions that are more fully theatrical (i.e., memorized lines, and a schematic stage set in accordance with script directions). In the latter mode, the characters may begin as though reading from the script, then show their independence, but return to the script at a later moment of doubt and hesitation.

Nothing about the presentation should betray a desire to divert or be liked by the audience. *Storyteller* takes control from the first moment. It is up to everybody else to come to terms with her. Similarly, Young Woman is much too intent on her own purposes and needs to care about audience reaction. Gestures and "stage business" should be spare, well thought out, and, of course, in keeping with character. In essence, this brief episode should be played with the intensity and gravity one would bring to the pivotal scene of a larger tale. (Which, of course, it is.)

Bedtime Story

A wintry tale in one chilling act

Characters

YOUNG MOTHER
HER CHILD
OLD WOMAN OF THE WOODS
MOUSE
STEPMOTHER
OLAF, *a brave boy*
MARIE, *a clever girl*
WEIRD LITTLE MAN (WLM)
GIANT

SETTING: *The child's bedroom + scenes read or imagined*
THE TIME: *Tonight.*
AT RISE: *Child sitting up in bed. Mother in a nearby chair.*

CHILD:	I'm ready for my story . . . [*Waits*] Mom—I said I'm ready—
MOTHER:	—For your story. Why don't *you* start a story tonight? I don't know where my mind is.
CHILD:	Once upon a time . . .
MOTHER:	Haven't I heard that one before?
CHILD:	[*Giggling*] A long time ago.
MOTHER:	How long ago?
CHILD:	Mother! Stop interrupting! A long, *long* time ago. There was a—naw! A long time ago there was, oh,

27

there was a big dark woods and a little house right in the middle of it. Don't ask me how I know it was right exactly in the middle of the woods! If it's my story, it can be. Mother! Are you falling asleep! No fair! *You* finish the story!

MOTHER: And right in the middle of this little house that was right in the middle of the woods, there was an old woman fast asleep.

CHILD: Bet she's a witch! I hope so!

MOTHER: She was having a lovely dream. In this dream—

CHILD: I don't care about her lovely dream. Make something happen already!

MOTHER: Suddenly something happened! She felt something furry on the tip of her nose. It was something furry that looked back at her with tiny red eyes when she opened her own eyes.

MOUSE: I'm SO hungry! I'm SO cold. Feed me and let me snuggle under the covers with you.

OLD WOMAN: You useless little thing, why should I feed you? Why should I keep you warm? Anyhow—it's much too early in the morning and there's only one scrap of bread left in the house.

MOUSE: We could share the scrap of bread.

OLD WOMAN: Off my nose this moment or I will do something terrible!

MOTHER: The mouse still balanced himself on the tip of the old woman's nose, rather cleverly, and tried to decide how serious she was about doing something terrible. Umm. Umm. . . .

CHILD: Meanwhile, some place else . . . like maybe at the far edge of the edge of the woods . . .

MOTHER: Meanwhile, at the edge of the woods there was another house, not much bigger than the old woman's.

CHILD: The old witch's! Was her nose green? Witch's noses are sometimes green.

MOTHER: In this other house at the edge of the woods, a boy was putting on his shoes and his brave face.

STEPMOTHER: Olaf! Haven't you put your shoes on yet! Lazy fellow!

MOTHER: That was his stepmother, as you've probably guessed.

CHILD: His really mean stepmother!

STEPMOTHER: Well, it's about time! Now: do you remember what I told you? What did I say?

OLAF: You said I should follow the middle path in the woods as far as it goes. I've never been that far. I don't know anybody who has.

STEPMOTHER: And what did I tell you to do when you reached the end of the path?

OLAF: I should fill the big sack with firewood. You said the best firewood of all is there.

STEPMOTHER: And don't come back without the whole sack full. It will be even colder tonight. I can feel it in my bones.

OLAF: Do I have to go that far into the woods?

STEPMOTHER: Hah! Don't tell me you're afraid! A big boy like you! Should I tell your father that his son is too lazy or too scared to fetch the firewood! Doesn't your father have trouble enough!

CHILD: Are you sure his name was *Olaf*?

MOTHER: That's what it says here, Pumpkin. [*MOTHER is now holding and reading from an oversized book that has suddenly appeared.*] So Olaf leaves his house and starts walking into the woods, making sure to keep his brave face on straight.

CHILD: Like *this*?

MOTHER: I said a *brave* face, not a *funny* face! Well, Olaf has only taken a few steps into the woods when he remembers that he has forgotten to take the big sack. He goes back to the house and opens the door quietly so that maybe his stepmother won't see that he's made a mistake. But to his surprise, he sees that his stepmother is not alone.

CHILD: Does it say in the book that there was a weird little man in the kitchen with her? A weird little man wearing his weird little clothes and doing a weird little dance?

MOTHER: If that's what you want the book to say . . .

WLM: [*Dancing and spinning*] I am the dancer! I am the spinner! Can you dance like this? Nobody can! Can you spin like this? Only me! Only me!

MOTHER: So there was the Weird Little Man, dancing and spinning and singing, and there was the stepmother standing very quietly with her eyes cast down and a hand over her mouth as though to keep the words from coming out. Olaf ducked in very quickly, snatched the sack, and headed back to the woods again without anyone seeing him.

OLAF: [*Walking through the woods*] A weird little man in our kitchen! There's so much I don't know about the world. Maybe I will learn something today. But—what's that noise? It sounds like a monster coming! It sounds like ten monsters coming!

MOTHER: Meanwhile, back in the middle of the bed in the middle of the room in the little house in the middle of the woods—

MOUSE: But you've given me *all* of the bread, the whole big scrap. Don't you want any for yourself?

OLD WOMAN: It's no use, Mousie. You have sharp little teeth. I hardly have any teeth at all, and the ones that are left aren't strong enough to crunch that stale bread. You may as well have it all.

MOUSE: Mmmm! [*Crunching sounds*] Delicious! And it's so much warmer here under the covers.

OLD WOMAN: Ah, in this world it's better to be a starving little mousie than an old woman. I can keep you warm, but there's no one to keep me warm.

MOUSE: You have a point there. By the way, are you quite sure there's no jam for the bread?

CHILD: She doesn't sound half-bad for a witch. But I want to know about Olaf and the ten monsters.

MOTHER: You'll find Olaf squeezed into the notch of a tree, hoping the ten monsters won't find him. He can hear enormous feet crashing through the woods. Now colossal hands are moving the trees apart, and Olaf beholds—

OLAF: [*Whispering*] A giant! Huge as ten regular monsters! He could crush me between his fingers like a bug!

CHILD: Oooh! Icky!

GIANT: [*Standing still and sniffing the breeze*] Fee! Fi! Fo!

OLAF:	[*To himself*] Fum!
GIANT:	Fee! Fi! Fo! Um . . . Fi! Fo! Ah . . .
OLAF:	[*Louder than he intended*] Fum!
GIANT:	That's it! That's it! Fee! Fi! Fo! *Fum!*
OLAF:	Uh-oh. I'm in for it now!
GIANT:	All right—Who said *fum?*
OLAF:	I . . . I did.
GIANT:	[*Searching through his pockets*] *You* did. So *you* did! And who are *you?* Who are *you* to say *fum!* to me? Ah! [*The GIANT has found his thick glasses and put them on*] I'll teach *you* to say *fum!* to me!
CHILD:	I don't know about this Giant.
MOTHER:	And meanwhile—
CHILD:	Just how many meanwhiles do you have? [*Yawns sleepily*]
MOTHER:	Meanwhile on the very *other* side of the woods a little girl is walking all by herself. She is carrying a basket on her arm filled with good things to eat.
CHILD:	And her name, I suppose, is Little Red Riding Hood! Really, Mother!
MOTHER:	Wrong, Know-It-All! Her name is Marie, and it is a straw bonnet she is wearing on her head, not a little red riding hood.
MARIE:	I would have nothing to wear it for, anyway. A little girl like me in this remote and impoverished sector of the provinces doesn't exactly have a silver pony at her service, and even if bicycles had already been invented, I wouldn't have one of those either.
CHILD:	Marie's a wise-ass.
MARIE:	Takes one to know one. Can I get on with the story now?
CHILD:	That's the whole idea, isn't it? So, tell me, Marie, you going to grandmother's house?
MARIE:	[*In genuine surprise*] Grandmother's house? You must be kidding? Haven't you heard what's happened to all the—well, never mind.
MOTHER:	Marie has been walking through the woods for a long time, so she's getting tired and cranky, and her feet are starting to hurt.

MARIE:	I'm going to plop down on the next rock I find.
MOTHER:	So she does.
MARIE:	Whew! I'd really like something to eat, too, but everything in the basket is supposed to be a gift. And I don't even know who for. [*Looking around*] Do you suppose this is the exact, precise middle of the woods? That's where I'm supposed to open the basket and read my instructions.
WLM:	[*Suddenly leaping out from behind a gnarled old tree*] It's for me! It's for me! The basket's for *me!*
MARIE:	Oh! What a weird little man you are!
CHILD:	Rumplestilskin's brother!
WLM:	Give me the basket! It's mine!
MARIE:	Your name is Rumplestilskin or something like that. Now go away!
WLM:	My name is nothing like that, and if you don't give me that basket I'll grab it anyway!
MARIE:	Can't catch me! Can't catch me, weird little man! [*She races through the woods*]

The scene changes

MOUSE:	Are you dying, Old Woman?
OLD WOMAN:	I'm trying to. I'm not even very good at that.
MOUSE:	Were you always so old and useless?
OLD WOMAN:	Heavens, no! I was once young and useless. Useless didn't matter, then, because I was a sweet and lovely thing. *Old* and useless is something else!
MOUSE:	Make a wish.
OLD WOMAN:	Go on. Don't talk crazy, Mouse. Just go away and let me die.
MOUSE:	Make a wish—try it.
OLD WOMAN:	Don't be cruel. I don't believe in all those old wives' tales even, though, yes, I was an old wife.
MOUSE:	You have been kind to me and I am magic enough to grant you one wish. Go ahead, try it. What do you have to lose?
OLD WOMAN:	One wish, eh? [*Chuckling*] One wish. . . .

Scene change

MARIE:	[*Still running, huffing, and puffing*] Whew! Wonder if that weird . . . puff . . . little . . . huff . . . man is still . . . huffpuff . . . chasing me. Oh, my God! Look at that! Will you look at *that?*
CHILD:	Look at what?
MARIE:	It's like a fairy tale! A house made of gingerbread and frosting with jelly beans and all kinds of good stuff! And I bet this is the precise, exact middle of the woods, too! [*She approaches the house*]
CHILD:	Be careful, Marie!
OLAF:	Be careful, Marie!
MARIE:	How come everybody knows my name!
OLAF:	It's a trick. It's a trap.
MARIE:	[*To herself*] He is cute! I wonder if he has a girl? [*To OLAF*] Where did you come from?
OLAF:	The other side of the woods. I was suppose to gather firewood here, but first there was this weird little man in my stepmother's kitchen—
MARIE:	Weird little man . . . hah!
OLAF:	And then a giant huge as ten monsters. He had trouble seeing me because his huge giant breath kept steaming up his glasses, and then when he had me in the palm of his hand—I mean, *really* in the palm of his hand—he just wanted to talk and talk and talk.
MARIE:	Well, the gingerbread and the frosting and the jelly-beans look real enough to me. If you were a brave boy, you'd break off a piece for me.
OLAF:	But it's a trap!
MARIE:	I guess you only *look* like a brave boy!
OLAF:	I know I shouldn't be doing this, but . . . [*He restores his brave face and moves close to the house*]
MARIE:	Break off a piece with frosting on it, right next to the door. No—wait, pick that candy apple for me, the one up there. Well—are you going to pick it or—

In a flash, the door swings open, and the OLD WOMAN snatches up both children and pushes them inside the house

OLAF:	Oh, no! Just as the Giant said!
MARIE:	Well, you could have been more careful! I didn't tell you not to be careful!
OLD WOMAN:	So, so. What have we here? Two little darlings. A boy darling and a girl darling.
MARIE:	Let us go. We didn't do anything to you.
OLD WOMAN:	Trying to pick the forbidden candy apple is doing nothing? You would have eaten my house down to the ground if you had the chance. Such little darlings. And what might be your darling names.
OLAF:	[*Whispering to MARIE*] You're not supposed to give your right name in situations like this.
MARIE:	My name is, ah, Gretel. Gretel von Strudelheim. And I have important friends.
OLAF:	And I am called Hansel. My father kills witches for a living, but I might ask him to spare you if you were nice to us.
OLD WOMAN:	Gretel and Hansel? Hansel and Gretel. Such darlings. And with such important friends and such murderous fathers.
CHILD:	[*Sleepily*] So that's where Hansel and Gretel came from . . . I never knew the whole story . . . [*yawn*]
MARIE:	What are you going to do to us?
OLD WOMAN:	Anything I want to. Anything! I have been given magical power over all who come to the middle of the woods.
OLAF:	Let's make a run for it!

OLAF and MARIE try to run, but the OLD WOMAN gestures at their feet and they are unable to move

MARIE:	[*Sobbing*] Here, take my basket instead. It's full of very good things that will taste much better than me.
OLD WOMAN:	[*Takes basket and opens it*] Hah! Are these the very good things that you have been carrying through the woods? Nothing but stones!
MARIE:	Stones! Everybody's tricking me! You can't count on anybody!
OLD WOMAN:	And this note. Here, read it aloud, little darling, my eyes are not what they used to be.

MARIE:	"Sorry, Kiddo. This is all that's left after taxes. In the middle of the woods you will probably meet a disgusting old witch who will eat you up and that will be that. Maybe we'll make some fresh children next year if things look up. Not your fault. You just picked the wrong time and place to get yourself born."
OLAF:	Wow, that's tough! I thought I had it bad.
OLD WOMAN:	We all have it bad. But I'm the one with the power now. And I can save you from a whole lifetime of bad things.
OLAF:	I thought I was supposed to have a whole lifetime of *good* things.
MARIE:	No, I'm too young to die! I'm still waiting to have my ears pierced!
OLAF:	And, gosh, I've never even shaved.
OLD WOMAN:	But this is the kindest thing I can do for you. Look at my wrinkled face.
OLAF and MARIE:	Ugh!
OLD WOMAN:	Look at these dark splotches all over my skin!
OLAF and MARIE:	Double Ugh!
OLD WOMAN:	And look at how I am stooped over, and how slowly and painfully I move, and—
OLAF:	We get the picture.
OLD WOMAN:	But it's all much worse than you little darlings can understand. People say mean things about you. Nobody wants to be with you and nobody wants to know what you think of things and nobody cares if you won a blue ribbon at the fair for baking tarts and nobody cares if inside your skin there is still a pretty young woman who wants to live and love. And nobody keeps you warm at night.
MARIE:	[*Genuinely horrified*] Could something like that—happen—to *me?*
OLD WOMAN:	[*Gently*] I was much like you. [*OLAF and MARIE gaze thoughtfully, first at OLD WOMAN, then at each other*]
OLAF:	Gee, I don't know.
MARIE:	It almost seems better not to grow up and get old and be treated that way.

OLAF:	You might even grow up to a mean stepmother who sends boys out into the scary woods.
MARIE:	I suppose I do have the potential. . . .
MOUSE:	[*Rushing in, agitated*] They're coming! They're coming!
OLD WOMAN:	Who's coming?
MOUSE:	Everybody!

Released from their magic paralysis, OLAF and MARIE dash to the windows

OLAF:	The Giant is coming. Only—only he's smaller. And getting smaller all the time. He's only as big as five monsters now.
MARIE:	There's the Weird Little Man! But, look, he's getting a little bigger all the time! And there's a mean-looking lady I don't want to know!
OLAF:	That must be my stepmother. And there are still other people coming.
MARIE:	From all over! What a collection—wizards and fools and a princess on a silver pony I could die for!
OLD WOMAN:	[*To MOUSE*] Don't tell me you didn't have a paw in this! Explanation, please!
OLAF:	And they are all of them coming right here, and they are all of them changing as they come. They're getting more—more—
MARIE:	More normal. More disgustingly normal.
MOUSE:	There's still time, Old Woman. Still time to shove the little darlings into the oven. You still have the time and the magic.
OLD WOMAN:	Oh, yes, I had almost forgotten. The power, the magic, the oven. My *revenge.*
OLAF:	[*Shouting through the window*] Giant—what's happening to you? You're not a giant any more!
GIANT:	[*Heard approaching the house*] Fee! Fi! Fo! Ah . . . Um. . . .
OLAF:	*Fum!*
GIANT:	Fum! [*Panting*] I've come to tell you. I've come to get it all written down. No more giants. No more elves. No more wizards. No more . . . magic.

MOUSE:	[*To OLD WOMAN*] Hurry! The oven is ready. Grab the little darlings before it's too late!
MARIE:	[*Turning to MOUSE*] Is this true? Is the magic running out?
WLM:	[*Larger now, and squeezing with great difficulty through the window*] Uhhh! I will never get used to being so big and clumsy! Yes, the magic is failing rapidly. But perhaps I still have some left. Watch me dance and spin and cast a spell. I am dancing! I am spinning! Ah, who can dance as I—oops! [*Staggers, and falls. Speaks tearfully from the floor*] Gone! I can feel all the magic leaving me. Leaving the woods. Leaving the world.
GIANT:	[*Now a normal sized adult, standing in the doorway*] You have to write it down, before everybody forgets. Write it all down for us, Jack.
OLAF:	My name's not Jack, remember? I'm Hansel. I mean, Olaf.
MOUSE:	[*To OLD WOMAN*] Shall I help you toss them *all* in the oven? I still have a little magic left.
WLM:	Why must it end like this? *Don't* let it end like this!
GIANT:	We have suffered so much just to become stories for you. Don't forget us! Please—don't forget us!
OLAF:	*I'll* write all your stories so you'll never be forgotten— if the witch doesn't eat me first.
MARIE:	Me, too. And I am probably much the better writer, so the witch should at least save me for last. Come to think of it—if you eat us both there will be nobody to write *your* story, too!
OLD WOMAN:	True. And to tell the truth: I no longer seek revenge. It was grand to feel the power for a moment. Ah, what a feeling! But leaving you little darlings to live a long life will be revenge enough. I would rather use my last little wisp of power as though [wistfully] I were a goddess of love.
MOUSE:	So be it! [*OLD WOMAN is instantly transformed into a young Goddess of Love, with toga, open to the waist, and floral wreath in her long, flowing hair*]
OLD WOMAN:	Now, that's more like it! [*All cheer her transformation and gather about. The room and the garden around the house quickly fill with other former fairy tale characters*

	who gather around] Hansel and Gretel, or Olaf and Marie, or whatever you little darlings call yourselves—do you hereby and most solemnly agree to keep us alive forever through your stories.
OLAF:	We sure do! You bet—and thanks for not eating us.
OLD WOMAN:	Not eating you? Oh—you must write that I did try very hard to eat the two of you. That will make it a better story.
OLAF:	You've got it, Old Woman—or Goddess of Love, whatever.
OLD WOMAN:	[*To MARIE*] And as for you—I have something very special to ask.
MARIE:	I'll do it!
OLD WOMAN:	Approach me slowly and keep your eyes directly fixed on mine. Open your heart, and your mind as you take every step toward me. Open your heart. Open your mind. And forget all the fear you once had of me.
MARIE:	[*Approaching OLD WOMAN slowly, step by step*] I am opening my heart. I am opening my mind. I am trying to forget all the fear.

GIANT, WEIRD LITTLE MAN, MOUSE, and all the other beings join hands in a circle around MARIE and OLD WOMAN, and close their eyes

OLD WOMAN:	In a moment I will reach my hands out to you. You will place your hands in mine. At that instant all my powers of love will flow into you. All the love I could not share, all the love that a goddess carries inside her while the world sees her as becoming only a frightening old crone. Keep this love with you through all your life, and add to it each day.
MARIE:	How do I do that? I mean, how do I add to the love you are giving me?
OLD WOMAN:	Why, very easily, child. By giving this love to others, young and old, mean and nice. . . .
GIANT:	Real or make-believe. . . .
WLM:	Attractive or despised. . . .
MOUSE:	All the magic that's left in the world: you have it now.

OLD WOMAN reaches out her hands. MARIE takes them. The beings immediately disappear, including the Goddess/Old Woman

NOTEBOOK

We embark on this perilous journey every night: from the comfort of familiar faces, objects, and routines to the dark shadows of sleep and the phantoms of dream. A beguiling voice whispers: "Forget the cares and rules of the day! Enter your very own land of enchantment where the only rule is to indulge your wishes." Nevertheless, one may be uneasy. There are moments in which our fears rather than our wishes gain ascendance, trapping us in a private theater of horror. Furthermore, a sentient being cannot unequivocally surrender consciousness. Even the young child is already sensitive to that other journey: "If I die before I wake. . . ."

Bedtime Story—and bedtime stories in general—provide a bridge of words and images to carry us across from wakefulness to sleep. The comforting words of family, friends, caregivers, and clergy—along with an infusion of friendly chemicals—serve a similar purpose when our bedbound travel has an even more formidable destination.

There are two other journeys in parallel progress as a child asks for her bedtime story. Day after night after day, she is moving from child to adult. Each interaction with a parent and each passage from day to night is charged with developmental significance. Her future self is being shaped by cultural, family, and personal narratives. She is not passive but, rather, a discerning and selective listener, adding her own gloss to the interpersonal texts. This life-course journey will be guided—and to some extent misguided—by the values and possibilities that are illuminated through close personal interactions.

The other journey is one that is being undertaken by the human race as a whole. We are moving—with reluctance—from the age of myth, magic, and mystery to the hegemony of the computer chip and the digitalized display. Indeed, the popularity of fantasy-ridden computer games attests to our unwillingness to surrender the ancient toy box in our heart's mind. Nevertheless, our universal heritage of myth, magic, and mystery is under relentless pressure. For example, how much longer will the fairy tales that nurtured the imagination of previous generations accompany us into the future?

We may think of *Bedtime Story* as a nodal moment in time in which the child's passage from wakefulness to sleep and the overtones of passage from life to death are set upon both by the bold shyness of developmental curiosity and the last thrashings of an endangered species—our fairy tale progeny.

You will have noticed that intergenerational distrust, abandonment of the aged, and several other disagreeable themes are at loose here. You will also have noticed that all of these disturbances are contained within the secure framework of the mother-daughter storytelling relationship. That this relationship is also subject to change with time as both continue their progress through the life-course is also evident. It would not be entirely amiss to regard the unfolding events in *Bedtime Story* as a lively exercise in preparing them to continue to accept and love each other as they will be.

Bedtime Story can be presented effectively with script-in-hand, token costuming and props, and well-selected moments of stage business. It also will reward imaginative staging—by that I mean staging that stimulates the audience's imagination as well as demonstrating the insight and flair of director and set designer.

There are casting decisions to be made. I like having the same person play Young Mother, Old Woman of the Woods, and Stepmother. The Child naturally becomes Marie. The parts of Olaf, Weird Little Man, and Giant could be performed by the same person, but there is a less intrinsic reason for doing so, and I think it's a good idea to spread the fun around. Mouse is best played by the most famous and unlikely person available.

For what it matters, *Bedtime Story* was written prior to Sondheim's musical *Into the Woods,* and we may confidently expect still other variations on fairy tale themes in the coming years as the resistance continues to a world of flickering electronic images.

A Month of Sundays

Characters

FATHER, *A middle-aged, middle-classed Victorian gentleman*

NELSON, *His son from his first marriage. Ten years old at first appearance.*

CHARLOTTE, *His daughter from his second previous marriage. Seven years old at first appearance.*

WIFE, *The current incumbent. About half his age.*

WORKMAN, *Brawny lower middle-class fellow, in his 30's or 40's*

ALICE, *The next child of Father and Wife. About five years of age.*

CHARLOTTE II, *She is now an independent, stylish and attractive adult.*

DUCKY, *Judge Timothy Ellis Duckworth, a debonair man in his late 30's or early 40's.*

CHARLOTTE III, *Still vigorous and attractive in her later years.*

NELSON, *Worn, infirm, and nearly gone.*

AIDE, *Lower middle-class male.*

The First Sunday

SCENE I: The Family Treat

A clear, bright Sunday afternoon early in this century. Slides establish the time with period photographs. Setting suggests a grassy knoll in the foreground with a well-manicured park extending in all directions. A ridge in the background partially obscures the ascending path.

Music: tiddly-tinkly salon piano.

FATHER: Over here!

A slowly moving top hat appears above the ridge, followed by the head and shoulders of a formally-attired, rather impressive (and self-impressed) man. His unhurried glance takes in the entire scene, and then fixes on one small gravestone among others. The children soon appear over the ridge. They are dressed in Sunday finery, each holding a bouquet and attempting in their individual ways to mask their apprehension.

FATHER: What a fine day The Lord has given us.
               What a magnificent view.

NELSON and CHARLOTTE are staring at their feet and stealing furtive looks at the gravestones.

               Nelson. Go to your mother.

NELSON stiffens as his name is called, hesitates as though hoping for a reprieve, then slowly approaches the salient grave stone.

               Nelson!

The boy proceeds under good control to the grave marker and places the bouquet.

               The lesson? The lesson, Nelson?

NELSON moves his lips, but cannot be heard.

               Speak up, lad!
NELSON: Mother died
               That I might live
FATHER: Continue—
NELSON: That I might live
               In the shadow of a saint
               A life of virtue and restraint
               [*Hurriedly*] Amen.
FATHER: Come along, then.

FATHER sets off down the ridge, without looking back. The children follow at a distance, staying close to each other. NELSON is stoical; CHARLOTTE fusses with her hair and outfit. Just when the children are about to disappear from view, WIFE appears at the top of the ridge. She is a young but drawn-looking woman, also Sundayed up, and wearing a sad little bonnet. We see her only from the waist up. She pauses for breath, looks intently at the gravestone for a long moment, then proceeds in the direction the others have taken.

Blackout.

Music to stroll by is heard briefly. FATHER re-enters downstage, followed by the children. New arrangement of gravemarkers. The children are curious about them but keep to their ranks. WIFE enters, remaining on the edge of the grouping, back to audience. FATHER guides children to the right spot, where they stand in semi-circle around another gravestone.

FATHER: Charlotte—go to your mother.

CHARLOTTE goes at once to her mother's gravestone and places the bouquet, rather proud of her neatness in doing so.

CHARLOTTE: God took mother
               Off to Heaven
               But I'm still here
               And almost seven.
               I live in joy and never cry
               And God knows all the reasons why.

CHARLOTTE glances at FATHER for approval; he allows her a nod and a faint, indulgent smile. CHARLOTTE then looks rather more urgently at small flat stones that are close together, near her mother's marker. FATHER walks over and touches her gently on the shoulder.

FATHER: Yes, why don't you . . .

CHARLOTTE removes two blossoms from the bouquet she had laid at her mother's grave. With affection and fear she places one of these on each of the smaller markers, sitting on both knees as she does so.

FATHER: Do you remember this lesson, too, my girl?
CHARLOTTE: *[Unsure]*
                One with a fever,
                One with a chill
                Were seized to . . . to . . .
FATHER: Manifest
CHARLOTTE: Ma-ni-fest The Good Lord's Will
                They sing with the angels all day long
                Because . . .
                Because that is where the best of children belong.

CHARLOTTE looks questioningly at FATHER, but he has no inclination to explain.

FATHER: What a fine day The Lord has given us.
                And what a fine family treat we have had.
                Now you two little scoundrels—you can march ahead
                and wait for us at the gate.
                Off with you now!
                But remember, today *is* Sunday!

The children move off briskly enough. FATHER watches them in amused indulgence. He then turns slightly to where he knows WIFE is standing, although he has not previously acknowledged her presence. This is enough of a signal for her to approach respectfully. We see now for the first time that she is pregnant. He offers his arm. She takes it.

FATHER: Damned hot! Damnably, beastfully hot!

FATHER fixes WIFE in a sexually possessive glance, then, in a gesture almost too menacing to be playful rubs his fist against her cheek. They stroll off together. Before exiting, she manages one enigmatic look back at the gravestones.

SCENE II: Later That Evening

A cloud-flecked moon floats over the rooftops of a Victorian street. Light rises in the children's room with its twin beds. NELSON and CHARLOTTE are dressed for bed; FATHER is magnificent in his smoking jacket. WIFE in robe and gown stands at the edge of the scene.

FATHER: Now.

Each child kneels by his/her bed.

CHARLOTTE: *[Confident, but mechanical]*
     Now I lay me down to sleep.
     I pray The Lord my soul to keep.
NELSON: *[Tense and hesitant]*
     And if I die before I wake
     And if I die before I wake
     And if I die—
FATHER: Nelson!
NELSON: And if I die before I wake
     I pray The Lord my soul
     to—take.

The children scramble into their beds. While FATHER stands back, WIFE walks to NELSON's bed and ties him into a restraint device. She offers him a sad little smile as though it is all she has left to spare, and riffles her fingers through his hair. She then moves to CHARLOTTE's bed, offering a smile and kiss. The girl accepts the kiss, but turns away from it slightly. FATHER offers his cheek for a kiss from NELSON, and then goes to CHARLOTTE where there is a big mutual hug.

FATHER: Good night, my devils!

FATHER exits; WIFE follows.

The children's faces are still illuminated by moonlight although their room is otherwise settling into darkness. Lights rise in the parental bedroom (bed area only is seen) as an oil lamp is lit. WIFE is already kneeling by side of their bed, facing the audience. FATHER rather ceremoniously moves to his knees, profile to audience.

FATHER:	Now I lay me down to sleep.
	I pray The Lord my soul to keep.
WIFE:	[*With real feeling and precarious control*]
	And if I die . . .
FATHER:	Woman?
WIFE:	And if I die before I wake,
	I pray The Lord my soul to take.

She slips into bed. FATHER extinguishes lamp.

CHARLOTTE: Nelson . . . Nelson, are you asleep already?

NELSON:	Yes.
CHARLOTTE:	[*Giggles*]
	Then you must talk to me in your sleep.
NELSON:	What must I say?
CHARLOTTE:	You must tell me—who lights the moon?
	And who blows it out?
NELSON:	Mr. Zweig, the lamplighter, of course!
	Everybody knows that!
CHARLOTTE:	My! He must have a long, long, long ladder.
NELSON:	The longest ladder in all the world.
CHARLOTTE:	My! I would like to see that ladder.
	I would like to climb that ladder!
	But I would get so dizzy!
	I would fall down, fall and never stop falling.
	Doesn't Mr. Zweig ever get dizzy?
	Nelson? Nelson!
NELSON:	I can't answer any more questions. I am really and truly asleep now.
CHARLOTTE:	Oh . . .just one more question?
NELSON:	Well, just one more. But not if it's about moons and ladders.
CHARLOTTE:	Nelson—why do they put you into that harness?
NELSON:	It's not a harness, exactly.
	It's just sort of a . . . I don't know.
CHARLOTTE:	They put horses into harnesses so they can pull wagons.
	But when they put you into that you-don't-know-what, you can hardly move!

NELSON: Oh, I can move a little. My fingers, all I want. My head, this and that. My feet, my toes. I just can't move the rest of me.

CHARLOTTE: But why? You still haven't told me why!

NELSON: It helps me to sleep. I think.
          That is what Father told me.

CHARLOTTE: Oh. [*She hops out of bed and inspects the harness*] Does this really help you sleep?

NELSON: Father also said, he said—oh, never mind!

CHARLOTTE: What did Father also say?

NELSON: He said that would keep me from doing anything wrong in bed.

CHARLOTTE: My! What would you do wrong in bed? How can any-body do anything wrong in bed except bathroom things [*giggles*] and we don't do that any more!

NELSON: That's enough questions from one half sister! Now, I am really, really, really asleep!

CHARLOTTE: [*Sincerely*] I know how to untie that harness, I bet.

NELSON: Better not. What trouble we could get in!

CHARLOTTE: Yes, better not! Nighty-night!
          [*Kisses NELSON and hops back into her bed*].

We now see only NELSON's face illuminated by moonlight as he lies strapped into bed. But we hear overlapping off-stage voices.

FATHER	WIFE
Now I lay	I pray The Lord
Down to sleep	I pray The Lord
Soul to keep	Down to sleep
Down to sleep	Down
Sleep	Sleep
Down	Sleep

NELSON: [*Struggles to raise himself, then slumps back. To him-self:*]
          What could I do—wrong—in bed? Cripes!
          I will never even have a chance to find out!

The Second Sunday

Bare stage. A brawny workman, sweatband around his temple, spades the ground with slow persistence. After a moment he stops to wipe his brow. Takes a long, forthright, unhurried look at audience.

WORKMAN: Well! Tut-tut-tut to you, too!
You don't like me working on Sunday?
Then stop dying for Christ sake!
Or take this spade yourself—
Here: who wants it? You? You there?
[*Bestows a good-natured smile*]
No, Governor, I really don't expect you to.
And I don't expect you to approve of what I'm doing or even to notice me.
We all have our place, I hear it said.
This is mine.
[*Returns to his digging, will occasionally visually inspect the progress of the hole*]
I like my job.
I know where I stand, what I'm doing.
And look, I'll let you on to something—
Do you think I do this all week long?
No, Sir! No, Ma'm!
Monday through Friday I dress fine and line my pockets with your money.
They call me a doctor, a surgeon.
Butcher the good people in the best hospital in town!
This here is just my recreation on a Sunday.
Diagnose you Monday;
Tuesday send you to the hospital;
Wednesday let the other saw-bones poke at you;
Thursday promise the cure;
Friday collect the fee.

A more grown-up NELSON enters, still dressed as he was in first scene. He observes WORKMAN and, in his hesitant way, wants to approach him.

WORKMAN:	Saturday is the Day of the Knife.
	And Sunday?
	Well, peace be with you, Governor!
NELSON:	Pardon me, sir, but—
WORKMAN:	Lad, pardoning is not in my line.
	Now, if I should begin pardoning
	Then, next thing you'd know,
	Every parson and priest would have spades in
	Their pretty little pink hands
	And this place would have more graves than all
	The surgeons could fill in a month of Saturdays.
NELSON:	Are you really a surgeon, too?
WORKMAN:	[*Sizing up NELSON, then slapping the youth's shoulder, and laughing*]
	Oh, you poor, serious young fellow!
	Listen, you can't go around believing
	Everything you hear, just because it is said by a
	Man with sweat streaming down his face
	And one foot in the grave.
	I can make up a story as well as the next person—
	You should know that real gravediggers
	Do not meet up with real Princes of Denmark
	We are but dull, cloddish fellows quite bereft of wit.
	I hope you brought your own entertainment . . .
	I can barely keep myself amused, and I don't
	Expect very much.
NELSON:	But you are in truth a gravedigger!
WORKMAN:	In truth!
NELSON:	[*Stepping closer to and staring into the grave*]
	In truth . . .
	It is not a remarkably interesting grave you have prepared here.
	It does not seem to go any place in particular.
	It could even be mistaken for—
WORKMAN:	—A hole in the ground!
NELSON:	No offense intended.
WORKMAN:	No offense taken, Governor.
NELSON:	Do you have anything somehow better in the way of a grave?

WORKMAN: Oh, I like that! What an aristocratic thought!
It might sustain me for weeks!
But no, lad, this is the best and only work I do,
As poor as it may be.
Gravestones, though! Lord!
You can have anything to your heart's desire.
The best and most prosperous stone-cutters
I can recommend to you.

NELSON: [*Turning away*]
No, I am really afraid not.
I had just been hoping there was somehow something better.
I know I should accept graves for what they are—by now—
But one keeps hoping.

Funeral music is heard. NELSON and WORKMAN stand back, the latter in a stereotyped deferential-reverent posture, the former more aloof and uncomfortable.
WIFE appears. She is pale, still dressed as in first scene, but no longer pregnant. She walks toward the grave slowly but without hesitation as the music continues. Music ends when she is a few steps away. WORKMAN offers his arm, but WIFE declines and, instead makes a circular let's-get-on-with-it gesture with one of her hands. NELSON is puzzled by this gesture, but WORKMAN knows what is needed.

WORKMAN: Music! More music!

All wait and listen . . . in vain.

WORKMAN: Come, come! Pipe the lady all the way! You may be paid by measure, but pipe this lady to her grave or you will answer to me! [*Brandishes his spade*]

Music resumes. WIFE nods in gratitude and proceeds with dignity to the grave and into the grave. Her bonnet remains visible for a moment until this, too, disappears. NELSON and WORKMAN exchange a glance of understanding.

WORKMAN: Don't tell me.
            Your mother.
NELSON: My third mother,
            For your earth.
WORKMAN: [*Admiringly*] She knew the way.
            That was a real lady.

The music again. This time NELSON and WORKMAN observe side by side.

FATHER enters. Takes a few, confident strides, then stops, turns around. WORKMAN frowns in disapproval, but NELSON gestures him to wait and see. FATHER takes a few steps back toward the wings. There he stands still a moment while the top hat is placed on his head. Now, properly attired, he sets out toward the grave again. When FATHER reaches the grave's edge, NELSON suddenly breaks from his aloof and impassive attitude—he rushes forward.

NELSON: Father! Father!
            I think I love you!

FATHER pauses an instant, his head and top hat barely visible as he has partially descended into the grave. He offers his son a minimal, rather begrudging nod of acknowledgment. NELSON is close now, his emotions unprotected, weeping, seeking a further sign of love or approval. But FATHER's head disappears into the grave. Only the top of the top hat is now visible.

FATHER: [*From the grave*]
            Nelson!
            Take this damnable hat!

NELSON does. Holds it in both hands. A "silence that can be felt" from both NELSON and WORKMAN. After what seems a long time . . .

WORKMAN: That's a wonderful hat, Governor.

NELSON raises the hat with the intention of placing it on his own head, but cannot bring himself to this assumption of power—not even with a second try. As he fails again to bestow the hat on his own head—music of a much livelier and skitterish character is heard. A little girl skips onto stage. She is garbed Alice-in-Wonderland style. NELSON is surprised and alarmed.

NELSON: Alice, Alice, dear—
                     What are you doing here?
                     Go home!
ALICE: Curioser!
NELSON: [*Very upset*] Go home! Now! This very moment!
ALICE: And curioser!
NELSON: Alice!

But it's too late. ALICE has leaped into the grave. WORKMAN looks into the grave, sets down his spade, wipes his hands on his shirt and trousers. Glances over cautiously at NELSON

WORKMAN: [*Much subdued*] It has been a long day, Governor.
                     Even for a Sunday.
                     Let me show you to the gate—
                     [*With sharp concern*]
                     You—you find some other place to be.

NELSON's attitude suggests for a moment that he intends to join the others in the grave. But he pulls himself erect. Suddenly looks more composed, and no longer a hesitant youth. Places the top hat on his head with assurance and walks off slowly. WORKMAN follows the departing NELSON appraisingly with his eyes.

WORKMAN: [*Hands in pockets, moving a few steps off. Stops to scan the darkening skies as though looking for something. Points to a place in the sky.*]
                     There, I suppose.
                     But we will be needing the long ladder tonight.

Blackout

The Third Sunday

A stylish apartment interior in the 1930s. Perky music of the period is heard from the radio. Furnishings include a bird cage with a pair of love birds (not real), and several potted plants (not real).

Door bell sounds.

CHARLOTTE: *[Off-stage]*
Let yourself in, Ducky!
And if you are not Ducky,
Keep yourself out!

Door opens, cautiously. DUCKY enters: a dapper man in his forties, tastefully dressed. He will speak with a cultivated, somewhat mannered voice. DUCKY holds a garden bouquet as well as a beribboned bottle of wine.

DUCKY: It is Ducky, and he is in.

He looks around the apartment. Obviously, this is his first visit. Strolls over to the bird cage. Makes little sounds and whistles to them. Now he noticed with disappointment and irritation that they are not real. Continues to stroll about, looking at knick-knacks and pictures. Inspects the most lavish plant and is again disappointed and disapproving.

CHARLOTTE appears: she poses in the doorway between bedroom and living room. Wears a sheath dress that shows off her attractive figure. She is neither a very young nor a very beautiful woman, but commands attention with her vibrant and self-assured personality.

CHARLOTTE: What a disagreeable expression on that gentleman's face!
DUCKY: Of course that gentleman has a disagreeable expression on his face. The lady he visits deserves a song forest of twittering and admiring birds. And what has she? But two budgies! And they are poor things of rubber that cannot chirp a note.

CHARLOTTE: [*Laughs*] I have a radio for songs. And for commercial messages, too! How many budgies can tell you what floor wax to buy between arias?

DUCKY: And the lady he visits deserves blossoms nearly as sweet as herself. Yet all her greenery was milled in Hoboken.

CHARLOTTE: Not true! Some are from New Rochelle.

DUCKY: Here! [*Offers the bouquet*] Real!

CHARLOTTE: Oh, well, how thoughtful. How thoughtful of you, Ducky. [*She accepts the bouquet in a courteous rather than a joyful manner, and soon sets it aside*] And a ribbon! [*Claps her hands*] I adore ribbons!

DUCKY: We must first have the wine. Then the ribbon is unfurled. Rules are rules.

CHARLOTTE: In your court, your rules. In my home court, we play by my rules.

DUCKY: Instruct me.

CHARLOTTE: First, the defense rests.

She leads him to a comfortable stuffed chair and eases him into it.

DUCKY: So, I am the defense!
But what should I rest?
I haven't done anything yet.

CHARLOTTE: That is what attorneys are always telling you in court, isn't it?
And you have done something,
You dreadful man-person you!

She settles down on the rug by the side of his chair. Arranges herself now, as always, to look just splendid.

DUCKY: The charges against me? I have the right to know.

CHARLOTTE: Why, you know them full well!
You have taken nine-tenths possession of my thoughts and now you sit here as though lord of the manor—just biding your time until you also take possession of my body.

DUCKY: Charlotte!

CHARLOTTE: I shock the gentleman!
He comes here.
To my apartment.
Lets himself in.
While I stand trembling in the next room
With scarcely a garment on my showered and lightly perfumed body.
Then he speaks passionately of seduction.
DUCKY: Charlotte!
CHARLOTTE: Or lets his wine and ribbon speak for him.
Oh, I know your kind—
Judge Ellis Timothy Duckworth! [*He cringes a little*]
Does that make you nervous?
To hear your true name spoken aloud . . .
[*Melodramatically*] here . . . in this private and secluded place where no judge has jurisdiction?
Come now, Ducky.
You must have been in many a secluded chamber with many a nubile maiden.
Why deny it?
You are just that kind of man!
[*She places a hand on his knee*]
DUCKY: [*Relaxing and entering more into the game*]
Since you are so perceptive, then—
Yes, as a rule I start a new woman every Monday.
Pick her out of the first session.
Defendant, plaintiff, jurist, secretary, reporter,
What does it matter?
She must simply be the most
desirable woman in sight.
CHARLOTTE: Tuesday?
DUCKY: Tuesday, she is already fascinated by me, and wondering desperately if she has a chance.
CHARLOTTE: Wednesday?
DUCKY: An occasion is found to look into her eyes, into the very depths of her soul—and also to touch her body in some way, so lightly, but one will feel her quiver, vibrate.
CHARLOTTE: What a wicked Wednesday person you are.

DUCKY: Thursday I just plain ignore her.
                Much too busy, you see.
                More important things on a judge's mind.
                She must have been mistaken in what she thought,
                Yet—no!—she could not have been mistaken.
                Her body and soul are quivering yet.

CHARLOTTE: Monstrous! The devils could learn from you!
                [*She leans over and admonishes DUCKY with an index
                finger in front of his face . . . and then slowly traces the
                finger along his neck and chest. Pauses.*]
                Friday? Oh, I don't think I can bear to hear of Friday!

DUCKY: [*Becoming aroused both by her touch and his own story*]
                Friday it is "I-will-see-you-in-my-chamber" day!

CHARLOTTE: Do judges really say that?

DUCKY: This judge does. And she will always come to my cham-
                bers, too. Always.
                Oh, don't expect me to tell you what takes place in the
                chambers, dear Charlotte.
                It's all classified. Classified and due process.

CHARLOTTE: You seduce her. Right there, on the spot!

DUCKY: No such thing! Justice moves with deliberate and deli-
                cious pace. Friday the rendezvous is arranged.

CHARLOTTE: I am tingling to hear about it!
                Poor, helpless woman, captive of her own desire!

*CHARLOTTE has slyly removed two wine glasses from an end table near
the chair and opened the bottle without DUCKY's notice. Now she places
a glass in his hand. Slowly fills his glass.*

[*With something like real desire in her voice*] You must fill mine.

*He does so. Now they are both serious. DUCKY guides CHARLOTTE to
her feet. They link arms gracefully and sip at their wine.*

DUCKY: Saturday was an agony of waiting.
CHARLOTTE: I know.
DUCKY: Today . . .

CHARLOTTE: [*Turns her back on DUCKY and walks a few steps away*]
Today is . . .
The day after Saturday.
DUCKY: [*Disconcerted*] I would have called it Sunday.
CHARLOTTE: [*Spinning around to confront him*]
Sunday! Don't you know what Sunday is, Judge?
Sunday is the Day of the Lord!
The Day for the Day itself to pose for its picture.
To hold still in the sunlight.
For good little boys and girls to stand as silent as stone.
And flesh and stone be as one.
DUCKY: Charlotte, you bewilder me.
CHARLOTTE: [*Sipping her wine again, lowered voice*]
Do you want to leave, Ducky?
Do you want to duck out of here, Ducky?
Run back to your pretty little wife and your
Pretty little children?
What do you want with a woman like me?
With a cruel, confusing woman like me?

In a rage, DUCKY sets his glass down, comes up to CHARLOTTE, seizes her by both shoulders and shakes her. Clenches a fist and shakes it in front of her face. Then, becoming aware of his actions, is momentarily paralyzed: angry and embarrassed. CHARLOTTE raises her face to him peacefully and sweetly, her eyes nearly closed. Takes his fist in both hands. Rubs it along her cheek, kisses it.

DUCKY: Charlotte. [*Her name barely escapes through his choked voice*]
CHARLOTTE: You are a dear man. And you shall have me,
Body and soul.
[*Presses close against DUCKY, arms around his neck, head against his shoulder*]
Body and soul.
RADIO: Friends, think of all
That your floor does for you.

CHARLOTTE and DUCKY remain locked in a gently swaying embrace.

Without your floor
You fall into your downstairs neighbors' soup!
This, Science has demonstrated.
And so, friends,
Don't be in the soup:
Be friends to your floor
And keep it shining with Waxoleum . . .

CHARLOTTE: Body and soul and floor wax
I promise you shall have all of me
Until midnight's last stroke!

She bites DUCKY's neck, then hoists the wine bottle with one hand and, with the other, pulls DUCKY, lurching gamely behind her, into the next room.

RADIO: "Oh, the music goes round and round,
O-wo-wo-wo- wo-wo,
And it comes out here!"

Blackout

The Fourth Sunday

Nursing home interior. Corridor with side rooms suggested.

VOICE: Second door to the left, lady.
                       If you're sure you want to see him.

CHARLOTTE appears. A good bit older than last time we saw her, but holding up well. Purposeful, no-nonsense manner. She is in heels, well dressed. Walks briskly, enters a room.

Lighting rises on room interior. NELSON is in bed, supine, asleep or worse.

CHARLOTTE: Nelson! Wake up!
NELSON: [*Softly*] Charlotte?
CHARLOTTE: [*Accusingly*]
                You have let yourself become a very old man!
NELSON: I am dying.
CHARLOTTE: I can see that.

Pause

NELSON: I said, I am dying.
CHARLOTTE: And I said, I can see that!
NELSON: Not very interesting, is it?
CHARLOTTE: It certainly is not remarkable.
NELSON: And it doesn't seem to get one
                Any place in particular.
CHARLOTTE: I have had enough of all this dying.
NELSON: And your rubber budgies—
                Have they died, too?
                Your plants from Peoria . . .
CHARLOTTE: Hoboken and New Rochelle!
NELSON: Yes, Hoboken and New Rochelle.
                Have they grown old and useless, like Nelson?
CHARLOTTE: Nobody has grown old and useless
                Quite like Nelson.

She settles on his bed and takes his hand in hers.

NELSON:	And your lovers?
	Are they still vanishing at midnight
	To be replaced by a fresh pony the next day?
CHARLOTTE:	Let's not waste time with trivia.
NELSON:	Good. I don't have the breath for it, anyway.
	[*Sinks back, exhausted and still*]
CHARLOTTE:	Nelson . . . Nelson!
	I just came here!
	All this way!
	Are you dead already?
NELSON:	Dead.
CHARLOTTE:	How dead?
NELSON:	Dead enough.
CHARLOTTE:	Talk to me a little, Nelson.

She is now sounding young and vulnerable. CHARLOTTE flutters in a shifting borderland between little girl and experienced adult.

> My, my. My, my, my.
> If you are not going to talk to me
> Let me at least talk to you.
> I have some questions for you, brother.
> They keep me awake at night.
> If I knew the answers, perhaps I could sleep.
> Nelson? [*No response*]
> Good. Now, listen carefully.
> Have you ever had a woman—I mean, ever?

A brawny, uniformed male AIDE has entered the room with his mop and bucket. His face will remain averted to us for a while. He goes about his business, mopping the floor, as he answers, as though for NELSON.

AIDE:	The old boy had three women.
	His mother,
	His mother,
	And his mother.

CHARLOTTE: No, you are certainly mistaken, sir.
He didn't have a mother.
Only three women who went silently to their graves
While he stood around with his thumb in his mouth.
AIDE: I hear tell he had a sister.
CHARLOTTE: Half of that is half true.
He had half a sister, and had but half of her. [*Gently*]
Even that was more woman than he has likely had, before
or after.
AIDE: But there was Alice . . .
CHARLOTTE: Alice? Oh, she didn't last long enough to count.
A spring shower, a summer rainbow,
And she was gone.
I knew she couldn't last—
But for a moment, yes, she did seem real.

*AIDE turns around. He is wearing a sweat band and the WORKMAN's
soiled shirt under his partial uniform.*

AIDE: Are you still furious about Alice?
CHARLOTTE: And the twins!
One with a fever, one with a chill
Were seized to . . . to . . .
AIDE: Manifest
CHARLOTTE: Manifest The Good Lord's Will
They sing with the angels all day long
Because . . .
Because that is where the best of children belong.
Nelson! I was the best of children!
Why didn't The Good Lord take me?
Nelson!
Oh, you really are being dead today, aren't you!
And how could Alice dance away so easily,
While I had to stay behind?
The fever didn't take me, nor the chill.

Music: faintly, a reprise of funeral music heard in second scene

CHARLOTTE: I couldn't walk dumbly
Like all mothers
Into the grave
And I couldn't dance into the earth with Alice.

Music ends

Nelson!
Please don't be so dead.
Don't be so useless.
Answer some of my questions.
I am so tired.
You don't know how tired your little sister is.

AIDE completes his mopping operations, and moves toward the door.

CHARLOTTE rests her head on NELSON's chest.

NELSON: Now you lay you
Down to sleep.
CHARLOTTE: [*Drowsily*]
Down to sleep . . .
NELSON: We pray The Lord
CHARLOTTE: Down to sleep . . .
NELSON: Our souls to keep.
CHARLOTTE: Down to sleep . . .
NELSON: And if we wake
CHARLOTTE: We pray The Lord
NELSON: Before we die
Perhaps The Lord
Will tell us why.

Pause

CHARLOTTE: Nelson,
Who lights the moon?
And who blows it out?
NELSON: Mr. Zweig, of course!
Everybody knows that!

CHARLOTTE: My, he must have a long, long ladder.

NELSON groans and stiffens.

CHARLOTTE raises her head, runs her hands lightly over his face and chest, as though undoing a restraining apparatus.

> There, Nelson. There, brother.
> I have released you from the harness.
> [*Kisses his forehead*]
> Whatever you do from now on
> Cannot be so very wrong.

CHARLOTTE slowly withdraws from the bed, then, with gradually increasing tempo, puts herself back in order, adjusting her hair, etc. Walks briskly toward the door. It is held open for her, respectfully, by AIDE. CHARLOTTE pauses a moment. Glares fiercely at him.

CHARLOTTE: I know! I know! [*In rage and frustration*]
> It must be me who's stupid! [*Pause, regains control*]

Lighting change: shifting, surrealistic colors

> Good Lord!
> Here I am,
> Wandering around for a month of Sundays
> And I still can't find the right gate!

CHARLOTTE walks off into a surrealistic distance, observed by AIDE as he leans against his mop. AIDE shoots an intense, questioning look at the audience, then quickly mops his way off stage.

Blackout

NOTEBOOK

Have you ever met a generic old man or woman?

Neither have I.

Many people object to having their personal identities submerged by age stereotypes. And rightly so. Why should a dim-witted number take precedence over all that this particular person has achieved and become? (Chronological age is surely one of the most dim-witted of numbers, slavishly moving up the scale one digit per annum. Let CA hold steady for a few years, or bounce backwards once in a while, and I might revise this opinion.) Social gerontologists agree that elderly people are probably less generic than anybody. It has often been observed that people get to be more like themselves with advancing age, and this means, of course, somewhat less like everybody else.

All this individuality has to come from some place. Childhood is the likely source. Locke, Rousseau, Freud, Monterossi and others have argued in their own ways that "as the twig is bent, so grows the tree." (And we sure have a lot of bent trees, don't we?) Today there is also more sensitivity to the influence of specific historical events and forces on the lives of those who move through them. When my father turns off the light after he leaves the room he is not exhibiting nonagenarian behavior—rather, he is being faithful to the code of conduct he developed when trying to make it as a young man during the Great Depression.

In appreciating the individuality of an aged person, then, we are learning to appreciate also the particular currents of time through which this person passed as well as the events and influences that converged on his/her most formative years.

Which brings us, sort of, to *A Month of Sundays.* In glimpsing the lives of Nelson and Charlotte at four points in time we may be honing our general sensitivity to the childhood and historical influences that contribute to the shape of lives in old age. To be most effective, the presentation should convey persuasive whiffs of each point in history (roughly—very roughly—from late Victorian times to just about now). History buffs will want to come up with just the right hat for Father and just the right bird cage for Charlotte II. Productions can be just as successful, however, if they just get across a sense of the period.

Some of the goings-on are not politically correct. They do reflect, however, the passions, anxieties, and hypocrisies of our recent past. An intergenerational audience is likely to have an especially vibrant time in discussing the events and relationships here portrayed.

Director and actors will need to feel comfortable with *Sundays'* blend of historicism and fantasy. Perhaps it is helpful to remind ourselves that history is parented, on at least one side, by fantasy, and that fantasy is also one of history's most exuberant offspring. In this connection, Workman and Aide should definitely be played by the same person (see if Zweig is available). Charlotte offers a provocative choice. One actress could take Charlotte all the way through. On the other hand, there is something to be said for other arrangements, e.g., a child and two adults of varying ages from a multi-generational family. Nelson from his first to his second appearance is not much of a stretch and can easily be a doubled role, and also carried through to the end. I would transform Father into Ducky, if only for the appealing nastiness of this doubling. Wife and Alice are best handled as single roles.

There is an underlying rhythmicity and musicality in this script that prompts me to suggest that the major roles might be best served with actors with some musical talent. Please find the cadences and shapes—the "big speeches" in particular are awaiting the melodic inspiration of gifted performers.

Yes, *Sundays* can be done as a script-in-hand reading, but it can yield a lot more satisfaction with at least a semi-staged production and will positively flower when given the full treatment.

Why Does the Fireman?

A One-Act Play in Four Alarms

Characters

OLD MAN, *He's comfortable with his old house, his old clothes and his old self.*

WALDO, *Sure, he's a great-grandfather clock—but whose?*

GERRY ATTRITION, *She's a brisk and youthful doc who understands everything except people.*

MADAME FUTURA, *A face on the wall? A mechanical marvel? She knows both more and less than she says.*

TIME AND PLACE: *Here and now.*

SETTING: *Interior furnished in yesteryear style. A checkerboard and its scattered pieces adorn a card table around which two chairs are to be found. At a rear corner of the room stands a majestic grandfather clock, its face to the wall. Near the other corner is situated a portrait of a silver-haired woman in Gypsy array.*

AT RISE: *OLD MAN slowly drifts forward through the audience, newspaper under his arm. Seems to be looking for something. Muttering to himself as he crosses in front of "portrait" [MADAME FUTURA]. She reaches through the picture frame and gently shakes the under-his-arm newspaper.*

OLD MAN: Damn paper. Never where it should be.
           [*Seats himself. Goes through ritual of finding the right arm-extension position so he can read the paper.*]

WALDO: [*Nonchalantly at first*]
           Tock-tock
           Tock-tock, tock-tock
           Oh, tock-tock, tock-tock-tock
           So!
           [*Looks vainly for response from OLD MAN*]
           So! What do you think you are doing?

is the clock the old man's conscience?

OLD MAN: It is possible that I am reading the newspaper.

WALDO: Hah! What is in the newspaper for you? The obituaries? Go ahead, look. See if maybe you are dead and buried. Stop the presses! Another old man is dead!

OLD MAN: The funnies, I'm reading. This Zippy, he is really something. And next the sports page—if you don't mind.

WALDO: Mind? Why should I mind? Go ahead. Read your precious newspaper.

OLD MAN: Thank you.

WALDO: Just ignore me.

OLD MAN: Lord knows, I'm trying.

WALDO: After all, why shouldn't you ignore me? I'm only your grandfather. I am accustomed to being ignored.

OLD MAN: Do you have to go through all that again? You are not my grandfather.

WALDO: Well, I'm somebody's grandfather! Not my fault I can't remember whose. So many years. So much moving around. Damp basements, dusty attics, eeeuch! Maybe I was better off in those basements and attics. What good is it to have a house when your only company is an old man who'd rather read Zippy than pay attention to his—or to somebody's grandfather.

OLD MAN: [*Glancing briefly at WALDO for the first time*]
           Did I hear you say you'd rather be back in the basement?

WALDO: No, you wouldn't! Anyhow, you couldn't! And anyhow, it's not polite to threaten a grandfather.

OLD MAN: A little peace, is that too much to ask?

WALDO: A clock. That's all I am to him! Tock-tock, tock-tock. Not appreciated around here. Definitely not appreciated. Look at me: a magnificent piece of handcrafted furniture. I could be in any museum.

OLD MAN: [*Gives up on the paper, wags finger at WALDO*]

You are not even a regular clock! If you were a regular clock you would tock *and* tick, and all the time, not just when you felt like it. And you wouldn't be forever sulking and nagging.

WALDO: Go on, shout at me. Why don't you kick me, too? Wouldn't that make you feel better?

OLD MAN: [*Making his way slowly toward WALDO*]

Oh, come on, Waldo

[*Touches him in a conciliatory way*]

I just can't take it when you get into those self-pitying moods.

WALDO: [*Bursting into stylized, overdone sobs*]

Well, somebody has to pity me! It's so lonely. Would you like to spend all of your after life in a mahogany cabinet?

OLD MAN: Beats plastic. All right, all right. What do you want from me?

WALDO: [*Brightening*]

How about a nice game of checkers?

OLD MAN: Checker, all right, checkers . . . again.

[*Returns to table, sets up the checkers*]

WALDO: [*Contentedly*]

Tock-tock. Tock-tock-tickety. Tock-tock.

My usual opener.

OLD MAN: [*Muttering*]

His usual opener.

[*Makes this and all moves for WALDO*]

My usual opener.

WALDO: Now the left corner piece. There.

OLD MAN: I was expecting that stupid little variation.

WALDO: Well, see if you were expecting this one—

DR. GERRY: [*From the audience, firm and loud*]

KNOCK-KNOCK

WALDO: I wasn't expecting anybody.

OLD MAN: Possibly, just possibly it might be for me.

WALDO: Hah!

DR. GERRY: KNOCK-KNOCK!

OLD MAN: Who's there?

DR. GERRY: Gerry

OLD MAN: Gerry who?

DR. GERRY: Geriatrician

OLD MAN: Gerry Attrition! Won't you come in, Ms. Attrition. [*To WALDO*] Watch it—we have company.

WALDO: Oh, I'm so nervous! Company! tock-tock, tock-tock, tock-tock.

DR. GERRY enters, a youngish woman with a professional look and manner. She totes an impressive attache case. OLD MAN offers her a chair, but she re-places him in his chair and starts to settle into the previously vacant chair.

WALDO: [*In a menacing, watch-dog manner*]
             Tock-tock Tock-tock Grrrr! Tock-tock

OLD MAN: Excuse him, please. He doesn't like strangers sitting in his chair.

DR. GERRY: He? Who? What?

OLD MAN: Oh, never you mind. Please make yourself comfortable, Dr. Attrition.

DR. GERRY: You can call me, Gerry

OLD MAN: Good . . . Gerry.

DR. GERRY: [*Glaring*] Doctor Gerry!

OLD MAN: Yes, of course. Doctor Gerry.

DR. GERRY: First, my credentials!
             [*Extracts a long computer print-out of her qualifications*]

OLD MAN: Bachelor of Science! Science of Bachelors!
             Masters Degree. ED.D., M.D., B.V.D. BVD?

DR. GERRY: Doctor of Bodily Virtue.

OLD MAN: Oh, yes. Well, very impressive, young woman.

DR. GERRY: I am writing a book. On old age.

OLD MAN: Isn't everybody?

DR. GERRY: Before completing my book, in the interest of accuracy and comprehensiveness, I want to observe one more old person.

OLD MAN: How many have you observed already?

DR. GERRY: Counting you, that would bring the total to approximately, ah, one!

OLD MAN: I certainly do feel important, Doctor!

DR. GERRY: I have a few questions for you.

OLD MAN: A few questions?

DR. GERRY: May I ask you these questions?

OLD MAN: Isn't that what questions are for?

DR. GERRY: Good. But I want to make sure first that you are perfectly relaxed. Are- you- per-fectly re-laxed?

OLD MAN: Am I perfectly relaxed?

DR. GERRY: Take your time. Just re-lax. You must re-lax so I can see which questions upset you the most, and what defects they reveal in your thought and personality. [*Bland, reassuring smile, looks at her watch*] Ah, you should be perfectly relaxed by now. First question: In what way are an orange and an apple alike?

OLD MAN: An orange and an apple? How are they alike? I can't afford either one of them . . . Can you, Doctor?

DR. GERRY: Why do you always answer questions with a question?

OLD MAN: Why not?

DR. GERRY: Why are child labor laws needed? Do you understand the question?

OLD MAN: Child labor laws . . . why are child labor laws needed? The laws are needed . . . so children can have the oppor- tunity . . . to work . . . 10 hours a day, 12, 14 hours, more. In sweatshops. In dirty, smelly places with no windows for the sun to shine in on them. Where machines bite off hands— just like that! . . . Child labor laws, yes, they are needed so the children can bring home a little money, and their mothers and fathers can pay the bills . . . to bury their little brothers and sisters . . . The typhoid, the diphtheria, the sweatshops themselves . . . A little money to bring over uncles and cousins from the old country. And the children can eat just enough to grow up and work and work and raise their own children who only have to work, so they can raise their children who don't work at all, but just sit in front of the television and grow old watching the reruns. Did I answer the question? My mind wanders a little, I suppose.

DR. GERRY: [*Taken aback, but bravely*] Let's try a little arithmetic. I'll bet you were very good at that. Here's an easy one. If it takes a man and a half two days to dig a hole three feet wide and seven feet deep, how many days will it take five men to dig the same hole?

OLD MAN: Oh, you are right—that is an easy one!

DR. GERRY: It is?

OLD MAN: It will take these five new fellows no time at all—the hole was already dug by the other gentleman and a half.

DR. GERRY: Ummm. That's not the answer I have here. Precisely how long would it take if they had to dig another hole of the same size? Remember, it took a man and a half two days to . . .

OLD MAN: Three months!

DR. GERRY: Three months?

OLD MAN: Three months. I guarantee you!

DR. GERRY: How did you come to that conclusion?

OLD MAN: You said five men? That's a committee! You've heard of committees? Three months—at the soonest. And even then, they might get it wrong.

DR. GERRY: I think that will quite take care of the arithmetic. Let's turn to history. What is the greatest invention you have ever seen or heard of?

OLD MAN: The committee.

DR. GERRY: Are you still working on the last question?

OLD MAN: The committee! I know it takes committees a good long time. But already they have dug a hole deep enough for all of us to fall into . . . entire cities. And the oceans and skies not far behind.

DR. GERRY: What is the greatest historical event in your memory?

OLD MAN: Florette Ruben.

DR. GERRY: Florette Ruben?

OLD MAN: Why do you always answer with a question? Florette Ruben, when she let me carry her books home from school. P.S. 35. That means public school, you know.

DR. GERRY: That was the greatest historical event?

OLD MAN: If it's my memory you want!

DR. GERRY: Perhaps we'd better go back to general reasoning. Here, let me ask you one of the classic questions.

OLD MAN: A classic question? I'm honored, Doctor.

DR. GERRY: Why does the urban, downwardly mobile chicken cross the road?

OLD MAN: Suicidal, I suppose.

DR. GERRY: Why do old people commit suicide?

OLD MAN: To get to the other side.

DR. GERRY: What do you think is the problem with young people today?

OLD MAN: Ah, the problem with young people today. Seenility, am I saying it right? Take a young person, maybe only 40 or 50. He, she, they're running around, looking for something. What do they call that, Doctor? Agitated behavior? Looking for something, but they've forgotten what. Forgotten, forgotten—ah! memory deficit! They've forgotten what they grew up for. Looking for their future. Now where did I leave it? Is the future back there some place, or is it still supposed to be out ahead, just waiting to jump on me? Or am I standing on it with both feet. Seenility. Ah, what a shame, what a disease.

DR. GERRY: If you could live your life over, what would you change?

OLD MAN: I would try to be . . . just a little kinder, just a little braver . . . I would try.

DR. GERRY: [Hushed and "sensitive"] And what do you think about . . . the afterlife?

OLD MAN: Ah, the afterlife. Well . . . it hasn't been so bad.

DR. GERRY: You know, I'm beginning to suspect that you have a sense of humor. Let me see. Sense of humor, Tests of. [Rummages around]

Here is a Famous Straight Line. You give me the Famous Humorous Answer: Who was the lady I saw with you last night?

OLD MAN: Once with a maid
I lived in sin (whenever possible)
Her skin at my touch
Bloomed like rose
Young, we slept a world from woes
And no thorn stung.

DR. GERRY: That's not the Famous Humorous Reply!

OLD MAN: And that wasn't last night, either, Lady!

DR. GERRY: I will give you another chance. Who was that lady I saw you with last night?

OLD MAN: [*Lost in his thoughts, at times with eyes closed*]
            There was wine
            Warm and pink
            Was her body
                Slow as the shadow a mountain makes
                Rising
                Her body curved through space
                Adventuring toward the first touch.
                Her body there was
                There was wine . . .

DR. GERRY: I don't understand you. Let's try once more: Who was that *Old* lady I saw you with last night?

OLD MAN: The old lovers have died their beautiful death
            To you remains the same door
            That, after hours in the rain and delirious with finding,
            Let them, drenched, laughing, stumbling, in
            The bed where whispering and all legends began
            That bare place on the floor where the sun still pours
            As golden milk for lost
            Children and lost
            Are the ways the cat had
            The old lovers have died their beautiful death

DR. GERRY: I'm very sorry, Old Man. You just are not making sense. You don't even remember my questions, do you? How long has your memory been gone?

OLD MAN: My memory has been gone for . . .
            [*Hides face in hands, shakes head, then, abruptly—*]
            Precisely seventeen years and three months to this day. I remember sitting by the kitchen window. It was warm. 89 degrees. That was before Celsius. 89 degrees Fahrenheit. I raised the window just a little crickety crack. And it just wafted away. I said to myself, "Yep, there goes my memory. It's just wafting away."

            I had just come in from picking carrots and onions. Seven carrots and six onions, three of them a little undersized. Ah, what a memory I had then. I could just remember and remember. You name it. I could remember it.

Oh, let's say, Boston in the World Series, nineteen-aught-three, the starting line-up. Collins, third base. A good man. Dougherty in left. Stahl in center, and Freeman in right, batting clean-up. Buck Freeman—skinny little fellow, but could he hit! Thirteen homers that year, best in the league! Then we had Parent at short, Ferris at second—and, say, do you remember the first baseman? Candy! Candy LaChance. He'd swing with all his might from the left side. [*Demonstrates*] And then from the right side. [*Swings again, and almost knocks himself out of the chair*] Just as awful both ways. He wasn't much of a hitter but then . . . well, I guess he wasn't much of a fielder, either.

That would be Criger catching. And he wasn't any great shakes either. But the pitcher! You know who that was? Cy Young! Yes, Mr. Cy Young himself.

First game of the series. Young is on the mound. And would you believe it, the Pirates nail him for four runs in the very first inning. But what do you expect, when the Sox make four errors behind him. Boston comes back, though, to win it in eight games—the Series went to five wins back then, and— Well, I can see you aren't any more interested in baseball than in carrots and onions. But I was just trying to answer your question, Doctor. Ah, once I could remember all those things—but damned if I can remember them now!

DR. GERRY: Old man, you have me thoroughly confused. I am obliged to tell you that there is something very much wrong with the way your mind works. Have you seen a physician? Do you know what's wrong with you?

OLD MAN: Yes, I saw this doctor. He explained it all to me . . . kind of.

DR. GERRY: Do you remember what he said?

OLD MAN: He said my arteries are hard. That's why my brain is soft. Depressing, very depressing.

DR. GERRY: Was there anything he could prescribe?

OLD MAN: Yes. The doctor prescribed a bottle of good wine. Cabernet. A wedge of succulent cheese. A soft bed. Chopin nocturnes. And a loving woman to share it all with.

DR. GERRY: The doctors prescribed all that for you?

OLD MAN: For me? Oh, dear, no. For himself. He was very depressed about my situation, you see.

DR. GERRY: I would really like to find something that shows you to better advantage. I'm getting depressed, too.

OLD MAN: Sorry about that.

DR. GERRY: Here is another Famous Straight Line. I'm sure you will have the Funny Answer for it. Why does the fireman wear red suspenders? Concentrate please.

OLD MAN: Why—why does the fire?
Why *does* the fire?
Why *does* the water?
Why does the blood shriek like firewater through an old man's bones, like a speaking tube, commanding him to—what?

DR. GERRY: Oh, why am I trying so hard? What do I expect from him? One more time, Old Man. Why does the fireman—

OLD MAN: —In the evening
When the uncertain thrush
finds it hard to sleep
And the electric beams refract from dust
He sits and watches the car lights
Blink on and off
Because he must
React
Because he must.
You ask: why does the fireman?
Because . . . There is still fire some place.
Because there is still something left to burn.
Why does the fireman?
Because he must!

OLD MAN's gesture and DR. GERRY's helpless frustration are frozen in a momentary tableau

WALDO: [*Just barely audible*]
Tock-tock Tock-tock Tock-tock Tock-tock

DR. GERRY:	[*To herself*] Old Man, you just don't compute. I don't know how I'm going to code you. I don't know what makes you tick. [*To OLD MAN and rising*] This clock—I don't know why I didn't notice it before. Say, this is quite an item! [*Approaches and admires WALDO*] I've never seen a grandfather's clock like this one.	WALDO: Tock-tock Tock-tock Tock-tock Tock-tock [*delighted*] Tock-tock Tock-tock
OLD MAN:	Not another one like it	Tock-tock Tock-tock
DR. GERRY:	Magnificent!	Tock-tock Tock-tock
OLD MAN:	That's your opinion	Tock-tock Tock-tock
DR. GERRY:	But—he's all tock and no tick	Tock-tock tock-tock
OLD MAN:	Waldo is ticked off today	[*Groans*] Tock-*tick*-tock Tick-tick-tick Tick!
DR. GERRY:	Waldo, I'm not sure that you that you compute either. Old Man. You can tell time, can't you? [*OLD MAN shrugs doubtfully*]	Tock-tick Tock-tick [*Slowing*] Tock- tick

DR. GERRY: You must have learned when you were young. About the little hand and the big hand?

OLD MAN: Yes, oh, yes. We had one big clock in town. When the little hand . . .

DR. GERRY: Good, go on!

OLD MAN: When the little hand was on its heart, the big hand was in your pocket. That was the clock on City Hall, you see.

DR. GERRY: You know, that almost makes sense. But come. See if you can tell time with your own Waldo.

[*OLD MAN tries to wave off this request*]
Give it a try, Old Man. I'm sure you can tell time.

OLD MAN: I don't think I can Not really. But
I will try for you. [*Approaches WALDO*]

Time: listen carefully	WALDO: Tock-tock
Time: let me tell you.	Tock-tock
Time: you're too damned slow	Tock
Your pendulum hangs around my neck	Tock
I get up at five-thirty with my heart	[*Droopy*]
pounding. I can't sleep and I can't wake	Tock
Ten hours later it is only 6 o'clock and	Tock
there is all the rest of the day to endure	Tock
Time: listen carefully	Tock?
Time: let me tell you	Tock?
Time: you're too damned fast	Tock-tock
You're tocking my whole life away!	[*Quickens*]
There are so few swings left to the	Tock-tock
pendulum . . . Slow down,	Tock-tock
Slow down	[*Slows*]
[*OLD MAN conducts the slowing tocks*]	Tock-tock
No, that's torture!	Tock
Dripping. Like water	Tock
Eternity has a leaking faucet	Tock
and it's driving me crazy!	Tock
Time: speed it up. Hurry it along!	[*Faster*]
	Tocktock
No. There goes my life!	Tocktock
Slower—faster!	Tock?
Stop!	[*Shrugs*]
Time: Go back—the other way!	
You can do it. Don't be stubborn!	[*Stubborn*]
Time: listen to me . . . Listen	

You see, Dr. Gerry. I can't tell time. Time won't listen.
You're the doctor. Maybe time will listen to you. You try.
[*DR. GERRY stands nose-to-nose with WALDO and tries to
influence him with gestures. Defeated, DR. GERRY backs
off. OLD MAN clutches at DR. GERRY*]
Time is telling on me!

Telling
Time
You can't
Tell time what to do..

[Unable to cope with this, DR. GERRY removes OLD MAN's hand, looks for an out, sees the "portrait"]

DR. GERRY: Ah, well, what have we here! This at least is something that makes sense. A portrait of a fine old lady.

OLD MAN: Look closer.

DR. GERRY: Why, it does look three dimensional, doesn't it? Artists certainly were clever back then.

OLD MAN: Ever been to a penny arcade?

DR. GERRY: Penny arcade? Do you mean . . . Is this a—say!
[With real enthusiasm, for the first time]
This is the real thing, isn't it.

OLD MAN: You might say so.

DR. GERRY: *[Admiring and excited]*
A mechanical fortune-teller! What an old beauty she is! Does she have a name, too?

OLD MAN: Madame Futura. Sees all. Knows all. Tells what she feels like telling.

DR. GERRY: Does she work?

OLD MAN: I expect so . . . for a price.

DR. GERRY fishes around for a coin. Approaches MADAME FUTURA who extends one hand in a stiff mechanical manner. In the same deliberate manner, MADAME FUTURA takes coin, crosses hands on her chest, nods. Then picks up oversized set of cards. Riffles slowly through them. Raises one eyebrow. Makes selection. Hands a card to DR. GERRY, then quickly resumes hands-crossed-on-chest position

DR. GERRY: Delightful! I've never met one of these that actually performs. *[Reads card aloud]*
"Stranger. This is a fortunate day for you. Money will come into your hand and then . . ."
And then? And then what?

OLD MAN: I suppose you could give Madame Futura another coin and find out.

DR. GERRY: Yes, of course.
[Does so. MADAME FUTURA repeats the performance, identical except for testing the new coin with her teeth. DR. GERRY reads the second card aloud]
"Money will come into your hand and then—into mine. It is

a fortunate day for me, too. Love and kisses. Madame Futura."
[*MADAME FUTURA blows a kiss at DR. GERRY*]

OLD MAN: What do you think of her?

DR. GERRY: She is amazing. I have to admit it. It's just incredible what they could come up with back then, before electronics. Truly a triumph of the primitive.

FUTURA: [*Enraged*] Primitive? I'll primitive you, young woman!

DR. GERRY: Why, you're a phony! And you're in on it, too, Old Man! You had me thinking this was a mechanical marvel. Authentic, old-time nostalgia. And what are you really, "Madame Futura?" Just another old woman! Shame! Oh, shame on both of you!
[*They try to look ashamed*]

[*To audience*]
There is nothing here of real scientific or historical inter- est—just a couple of old people and the world's nuttiest grandfather clock!

WALDO: [*Irritated*]
Tock-tock, tock-tock, tock-tock, *tock*!

DR. GERRY: [*Gathering her materials and stuffing them into the attache case*]
Old Man, thank you for your . . . ummm . . . hospitality. I don't want to tire you.

OLD MAN: Oh, I'm not in the least, You're welcome to stay.

DR. GERRY: Well, actually I do have to be going along. The book, you know.

OLD MAN: Yes, the book. Did I help?

DR. GERRY: I can't tell you how helpful you've been. Well, Old Man . . . [*Extends her hand to shake his*] I thank you and I wish you a long life.

OLD MAN: You wish me . . . what?

DR. GERRY: A long life.

OLD MAN: You do?

DR. GERRY: Why, yes, of course.

OLD MAN: You really mean that? Come back and sit down. That's the most interesting thing you've said yet, Doctor.
[*Reluctantly, DR. GERRY sits*]
How long a life do you wish for me?

DR. GERRY: Oh, long . . . long. As long as you want.

OLD MAN: Another ten years?

DR. GERRY: Certainly. More than that!

OLD MAN: Fascinating, Doctor! Another twenty years, then? Fifty years? Yes? Another hundred years?

And if I get sick, you'll help me pay my bills? and if I feel like working, you'll help me land a job? You'll let me use my experience as power, and let this power grow? Fascinating, Doctor!

DR. GERRY: [*Very uncomfortable*]

Well, why, I mean . . .

OLD MAN rises slowly and moves stealthily behind DR. GERRY. As OLD MAN speaks, he places his arm in an apparent hammerlock around her throat

OLD MAN: Or—won't you instead

sneak up

and strangle me in my sleep one night?

You do want me dead after all?

DR. GERRY: [*After a pause and, then, quite matter of factly*]

Right.

I do want you dead after all.

That's only natural, isn't it?

OLD MAN: [*Releasing his hold*]

Why don't you run along now, Doctor, and write your book. I think I really am getting a little tired.

WALDO: [*Hopefully*]

Tock-tock, tock-tock, tock-tock

MADAME FUTURA goes through her mime repertoire, but in an agitated and flirty manner

OLD MAN: And why don't you take these characters with you? They're tired of me, too. Go ahead. They'll make nice conversation pieces.

DR. GERRY: Well . . .

OLD MAN: And you can always kick them when you're in a bad mood.

DR. GERRY: Very well.

She gestures to WALDO and MADAME FUTURA. They follow her off stage, each with his/her characteristic walk and style

Lights dim

OLD MAN settles down at the table again, this time in what had originally been the vacant chair

OLD MAN: There! And you . . . you can go, too.
You have been patient.
But I don't want to bore you any longer.
I know that when your turn comes,
You will do old better than me.
You will have learned so much . . . with your books.

Well, what are you waiting for?
Go, go on with your lives.

I will be all right here.

I will breathe in, and [*slowing*] I will breathe out and I will breathe in . . . in and . . . I will . . . breathe . . . out, and then—well, you know.
Nothing of interest will happen here.

You go.

But, listen. If you do come back, make it just you. Never mind the others.

Maybe we'll have a nice cup of tea . . .

Maybe we'll play a nice game of checkers?

Turns attention back to the checkerboard

Lights fade

| NOTEBOOK |

Is old age a comedy or a tragedy?

The answer is yes.

And is the gerontologist an asset or an ass?

Right again!

Why Does the Fireman? has something to offend almost everybody. Those who never remove their pasted-on inspirational smiles may object to the indignities of old age being put through a vaudeville turn. Those who are dedicated to nailing old age to the wall as a clinical specialty or laboratory trophy may be provoked by Dr. Gerry's misadventures. And those who would just settle for a few laughs may be the most distraught: when you stop to think about it, it's not all so funny, is it?

This vaudeville of the absurd should be played with strength from Dr. Gerry as well as Old Man. She really believes in what she is doing, and is as reasonable a person as the situation allows. When she flares up in anger at the "subject" who is not meeting her expectations, she really does flare up. It is a real contest between the two of them. The audience must eventually recognize itself in her faith in the modern clinical/scientific mentality and her underlying anger and helplessness. Old Man is more than a squabbler and eccentric. His dignity is never compromised even when foolishness is rife about him. He's the guy who know the score. (And he absolutely has to know the players, too, as he does his "wafting memory" speech: it's only on target when he can actually remember all that he says he can't.)

Waldo and Madame Futura can define themselves as sharp-edged characters who compete for attention. Waldo gains in both poignancy and humor by speaking in an accent drenched in whatever ethnicity one prefers (Brian Mishara's original Waldo was hilariously Yiddish, but Southwestern Cowboy and New England Yankee have also been memorable interpretations). Madame Futura can and does properly steal the show when her unexpected mime routine has been carried off to perfection.

There are several critical shifts in level and mood. Old Man's response to "Child labor laws . . . why are child labor laws needed?" is the first revelation of the tragic vein as well as the first clear indication that he lives in a deeper world than Dr. Gerry. Old Man should just slip imperceptibly into this rumination, leaving it to Dr. Gerry and the audience to discover the new turning for themselves. From this point forward, a sensitive performance will limn the ambiguities and pitfalls as well as pratfalls. Certainly, we would not want to miss the search and assertion in Old Man's "Why—why does the fire?" or Dr. Gerry's sense of having suddenly encountered the limits of her (and our) mastery when asked to turn back the clock. The feigned murder scene should also be played "for real" until he releases his grip. The audience should believe that Old Man is actually about to rid the world of this helping person who wants him dead. In a superior performance, the audience will realize that Dr. Gerry has actually performed a service to Old Man by stimulating him to rediscover his own center of being.

Fireman needs its actions as well as its words for most effective presentation. Script-in-hand performance can be effective if it has been well rehearsed with respect to both words and actions.

Activities of Daily Life

Characters

REALITY ORIENTATION PERSON, *A woman of some years*
MR . . . AH-UHM, *A man of some years, plus some*
THE VAPORS, *Four aged people disguised as empty chairs*
GUS, *An attendant, similarly indisposed toward visibility*

TIME: *Not Just Yet*
PLACE: *Where They Get Put*
AT RISE: *The room is rather too brightly lit. It contains five institutional chairs and a portable chalkboard with the drawing of a clown's face. REALITY ORIENTATION PERSON (ROW) enters briskly, goes to the chalkboard, and selects a bold color from among the pieces of chalk available. She prints today's day, date, month, and year in BIG letters. Steps back to admire her work, consults her watch with some annoyance, then fiddles with the chairs until they are in just the right semi-circular arrangement.*

THE VAPORS and MR. AH-UHM (MR.) enter. They are obviously in no hurry. ROW hustles each to his/her preordained seat. She is working hard at being both professionally therapeutic and time-efficient.

MR. AH-UHM is the third person to be seated. Just when everyone else has been planted in a seat, he starts to rise again, and ROW gently but firmly presses him back down.

ROW: [*Whispering*] Gus, Mrs. Whipple did go to the bathroom, didn't she? Are you sure? [*To MR. and THE VAPORS*] Good morning! GOOD MORNING!! Good morning, Ralph Haslett.

Good morning, Selma Greenberg. Good morning, Mr. Ah-Uhm (what's this guy's name again?) Good morning, Edith Whipple. Good morning, Claudia Nims. Who knows what day it is today? [*Crosses to chalkboard, raps on it for attention*] Selma Greenberg, tell us all what day it is today. . . .
[*MS. continues with her reality orientation exercise, but we no longer can hear her. MR. AH-UHM blinks a couple of times. Looks about alertly, as though through a high window. He rises gracefully from his chair—and as he does—*]

Lighting change: Soft amber spot rises on MR. AH-UHM as other lights fade. As he speaks, a pattern of branches and leaves, gently touched by a breeze, is projected behind him.

MR.:   These trees, those birds
        I don't know their names,
        Names of insects I have mostly forgotten,
        In truth, I've forgotten them all.
        Try calling to them—well, it's hopeless
        A memory like mine makes it hopeless.
        For a long time I've done without it
        (How long I wouldn't know)
        Trees and birds and insects look scared today
        To me they look scared
        I think it's the names
        Try calling to them—well, it's hopeless
        I've lost their names and they know it
        A memory like mine makes it hopeless
ROW: [*Whispering savagely*] Edith, you did go to the bathroom!

Light and projections change: A sudden disruptive, convulsive effect gives way to a freeze-frame that seems a distortion or caricature of the original branch and leaves pattern.

MR.:   [*Turning slightly away, and touching his hands lightly to his temples*]
        These trees seem twisted in flight,
        Those birds seem rooted in midair,
        Even the insects have lost their way

I had not guessed they so needed me to know their names
A memory like mine makes it hopeless
I would apologize
Try calling to them—well, it's hopeless

Lighting change: All lights out except for the spot
Speaking more rapidly and under some pressure—

Just this morning or was it just this morning
On that one plot of land not yet built upon
I saw suddenly something leap from the dry earth so high into the
early sun's shimmer that it was as suddenly gone or perhaps that
was me
perhaps again pursuing the names
In truth, they've all forgotten me
Try calling to them—well, it's hopeless
The sun itself is stunned and helpless
A memory like mine makes it hopeless.

Music: Solo flute or oboe. Spot light out. Projection: A door slightly open.
MR. now speaks softly and as though from an increasing distance.

What comes after
After the being talked at
After the being walked off from
After the door closes as doors close in a dream
Soundlessly
After the empty room hears my apology

End music

I listen to the healing flow of silence around the wound
I feel the mouth of the grave at my mouth
All those words,
all those names
devoured so patiently, so without complaint

Spot follows MR. over his erratic path with his hands raised high, as
though selecting and feeding delicacies to small birds

I would feed this enormous mouth yet again
but with what meager crumbs,
what hazed memories, canceled addresses, voided names?
Here, death, sweet old child
Here, forgetfulness, swift cold child
Beg for your crumbs!

MR. pauses, shuts his eyes

There is in this no time time for everything
After the empty room hears my apology.

ROW: Do not groom, Selma Greenberg! Repeat—Do not groom. This is
not Activities of Daily Life. Repeat—Selma Greenberg, This is
not Activities of Daily Life. This is Reality. This is Reality Orientation.

MR.: [*Enlivened, opening his eyes brightly*]
A bird!
A bird!
I taste the touch of its wings
    It smells of damp spring days with more rain still to come
—My name?
Could be Chester. Could be.
Some people are Chester. Go ask Chester. He'll know.

MR. strolls about, in command, gesturing as he explains

The tree grows right through the bird. Right through.
And the bird grows right through the tree.
All the insects know their own names. Absolutely.
This is what keeps them in line.
A line drawn down the center of this room will keep going forever
at no particular speed to everywhere there is to go
So why are you still here?
Oh
You're not

Sound: Light percussion, rapid and intricate rhythms.
*Projections: Rapidly changing fragments of nature scenes. MR. speaks
with vibrancy.*

Crickets! Beetles! Moths! How
lovely, oh, how lovely!
Spiders! Scorpions! Lizards!
Finches flirting in the willows!
Grackles strutting on the wires!
A circus!
I, too, I too proclaim my name
and claim this life mine, all life mine
All colors, shapes, slithers, all eyes bright with the shined moment.
A windgift!
The names rush toward me
Irresistible, this dance
This music—when did it begin?

End music

Lighting change: To original brights

MR. sits down again, staring vacantly ahead.

ROW: [*Calling to the wings*]
      Gus, they're all yours! Come and get them!
      [*She quickly erases chalkboard and hustles off*]
MR.:   A leaf rises from the dry earth.

He gazes upward, then shuts his eyes

Blackout

| NOTEBOOK |

Consider first an agreeable story, then a disturbing fact.

The time came to create time and all the time-sensitive beings. One breath from God or gods brought the divine gift of life to the inert. Either the gods themselves or the humans they had enthusiated (impregnated with the breath-seed of God, i.e., entheo-ed) now had another crucial mission to perform. All that had come into existence must be named. In some versions of this near-universal story, it is the naming itself that certifies existence; a creature or even a geographical feature or force without a name cannot be said fully to exist. And just as the name creates the being, so does the namer exult in power over this being, feature, or force. Ernst Cassirer elaborated this concept in his anthropological philosophy—but we knew it already, thanks to Rumplestilskin. An agreeable story, then, and one that may help to explain some things even today.

The disturbing fact is one that has become increasingly familiar in our increasingly long-lived society. What goes first? Where do the irritating little drop-outs occur in that glistening memory apparatus we have relied on for so many years? The names, of course, the names. You and I are not so bad off. The person who is really having trouble is . . . uhm, Whathizname.

Activities of Daily Life is an invitation to enter for a moment into another person's interior dialogue, a person who knows that he is at terrible risk. As names melt away, so does the entire structure of meaning threaten to escape us. We become his witness during one of those frightening transitional moments between "normal decline" and obliviousness.

Becoming a stranger even unto himself, Mr. Ah-Uhm nevertheless retains a keen appreciation for what he can still taste of life. I didn't know how he would cope with this ordeal, but he found the answer—his answer, any how. If there is a primary vital essence to life and nature that is prior to words (as so many myths suggest), then perhaps this essence is also available to us if the day comes when the names and other words do not.

Can we more be sensitive and less managerial to those for whom even the activities of daily life have become alien? Can we even learn something elusive but crucial from their efforts to sink their roots into a nourishing reality?

Ideally, your Mr. Ah-Uhm would be James Stewart, more than a little befuddled, but still courteous, decent, and somehow discovering or improvising his own fragile course. In any case, he would be a soft-spoken but persistent person who is beyond any impulse to deceive himself or us.

Activities of Daily Life is most effective when Mr. Ah-Uhm has his lines securely memorized and has found their circling, but evolving rhythms. Presentation can be even more abstracted than what is suggested in the script, but it is useful to set forth a concrete reality (Reality Orientation Person and chalkboard) through and against which his spirit can wander. An alternative is to do ROW as an off-stage voice (which could be pre-recorded), and allow Mr. Ah-Uhm to wander among the audience, in a drifting but not entirely purposeless quest, speaking now to one and now to another member of the audience.

Where the audience mindset appears most inhospitable to *Activities of Daily Life* can prove to be the most compelling venue. Busy, schedule-conscious, goal-directed careproviders, policymakers, and the like may be in greater need than they realize of a confrontation with the melting-awayness of experience and with the sense of a something that comes before and after words.

Father Muncrief's List

Characters

FATHER MUNCRIEF, *An elderly man of ascetic and severe appearance.*
TESTY OLD WOMAN, *She is heard but not seen.*
FEMALE SINGER, *Live or on tape.*

TIME AND PLACE: *The aging town of Midvale. Now.*
AT RISE: *Bach's Gigue (Partita No. 6 in E minor) is heard on piano or*
   harpsichord.
   Photograph slides are seen:
   • *Distant view of a town in its valley or mountain setting*
   • *A closer view that brings the old church into prominence*
   • *A closer view of the church*
   • *Focus on bell tower. A human figure can just barely be seen*
   • *Closer still: the figure is that of a priest, bent forward, peering down*
   at the town. A rough circle has been drawn around this figure.

End slides and music. Lights rise on the bell tower interior. FATHER
MUNCRIEF is standing in the position displayed in the photographs. He is
not yet aware of audience. Despite his somewhat remote and forbidding
appearance, he speaks in a lively, childlike manner.

FATHER M: I see you! I see you!
           Midvale: I see you!
           You are not unobserved by higher authorities.

He notices audience and acknowledges with a nod, but completes his little speech to the unhearing town.

> I see the confession in Slotkin's delivery van,
> Parked, again, too far from the curb.
> I see the confession in the way that Mrs. Herman
> and Mrs. Carlson passed on the street
> As though each the other did not exist.
> I see the confession in Old Mr. Wigby's tight grip
> on the leash of his ugly and unfortunate dog.
> And I hear all the confessions rising up,
> Confessions for sins yet to be:
> What hopeful little sins!
> What dainty little sinners!

He moves away from the window and seats himself on a simple wooden chair placed at a small wooden table. There are two blank sheets of paper and a pencil on the table.

> Forgive me for sitting.
> Doctor Bloom wants me off my feet.
> All right, then!

Looks at the sheets of paper. Lifts the pencil. Writes one word on each sheet as he speaks.

> For. Against. All right, then!
> Firstly—For.

Stands up.

> No. Firstly is why I make lists.
> Why does anybody make lists?
> I could give you a whole list of reasons.

Realizes he is standing, so sits down again, making apologetic gestures to himself.

Reason Number One:
It is pleasant to make lists.
Reason Number Two:
When we pleasantly make lists
We cannot at the same time
Occupy ourselves with unpleasant thoughts.
But you say: what if the list itself is
A list of unpleasant thoughts?
All right, then!
Even unpleasant thoughts become more bearable
When they are made up into a list.
You see that, don't you?
By the time we get to "Unpleasant Thought
Number 17" we are already
Feeling better about ourselves
For having thought of so many unpleasantries
And having arranged them in such
An orderly way.
Suppose this is—what shall we say?—
The thought of the pain-killer wearing off
Before Doctor Adams has completed the drilling.
Happened once, could happen again!
But now, you see, now,
Doctor Adams' drill is no longer
A menace on the loose that can penetrate us
Whenever it cares to pierce our minds.
No, it has been tamed by our list.
It is simply Unpleasant Thought Number 17.
It will always be imprisoned between
Numbers 16 and 18.
Reason Number Three—well, never mind!
You get my point.
Lists are real and manageable
Even when nothing else is.
All right, then!

Stands, paces about, prompting and organizing with his pencil, as a conductor with a baton.

Firstly, For!
"Because it is all over"

Returns to the table, and, still standing, writes this statement on one of the sheets.

Number One, then: "Because it is all over."
Does this need to be specified further?
Not really. We all know what is meant.
"It" is everything that has come to mean anything.
That is the "It" that is over.
Oh? I mean: for me, of course. For me.

Moves to the window, crossing his arms on his chest

I don't really look down on them.
And they don't really look up to me.
But we all seem to prefer it this way.
Habit, I suppose.

Back to the table.

Secondly—For. Or: firstly—Against?
I seem to be in a For mood at the moment.
Reason Number Two.

Writing on the same page.

"Because I have nothing left."

The voice we hear is that of a TESTY OLDER WOMAN (TOW).

TOW: You just said that!
FATHER M: Did I?
TOW: "Because it's all over." "Because I have nothing left." Same
           difference!

He muses over the list.

FATHER M: They feel like different reasons to me.
           Even if "It" wasn't all over, you see,

"I" would be over. Even if "it had something left,
"I" wouldn't.

TOW: Sounds like foolishness to me—but it's your list.

FATHER M: My list, yes. Not that it's anything to be proud of.
All right, then. Reason Number Three—For.
"Because it doesn't matter."

TOW: That's a "For?" If it doesn't matter, that's a "For?"
If it doesn't matter, then you could do it
Or you could not do it.
I wouldn't call that a "For!"

He has a difficult time deciding this one.

FATHER M: Why don't we just put that one in parentheses.
Just for now.

TOW: Why doesn't he just put himself in parentheses!

FATHER M: Why doesn't she just—no, that would not be charitable!
Perhaps it is time to start the other list.
Firstly—against.

TOW: Because it is a mortal sin.
That's the only reason you need, *Father* Muncrief!
And I'll tell you something—

He tilts his head and snaps his fingers a la Duke Ellington, and the voice abruptly stops. He listens a moment to be sure it's gone.

FATHER M: Reason Number One: Against.
"Because it would be such a pathetic gesture."

Writes this down on the other sheet. He then closes his eyes, folds his hands together on his chest, and listens—at first, to nothing.

It will start soon.

Music: "You Keep Coming Back Like a Song. (Ella Fitzgerald version). First verse is heard, music fades as instrumental interlude begins. He revives from his little trance vacation. Speaks in a different voice, a throaty roar of accusation.

"*Father* Muncrief! Who did you beget?
Beget? Beget?

        Who did you fashion from your loins and hers?
        Who did you hold against the night?
        The night? The night?
        Whose sweat did you taste?"

Back to his own voice:

        Because it would be such a pathetic gesture."
        By this I mean what would it end?
        What would it end that had ever begun?
        Reason Number Two: Hmm. Reason Number Two.
        Ah!

Writes on the second sheet.

        "Because it would upset the Church and the laity."
        And it would.
        But it would also excite them so.
        "Did you hear about that old priest in Midvale?"
        "The one who popped himself off?"
        "That's the one."
        "Must have been cracked."
        "Must have gone senile."

TOW: "Must have lost faith!"
FATHER M: She's back! Oh, well.
        Perhaps you can help me keep score.
        Tied right now, I believe. Two For, Two Against.
        But it is quality that counts, too, not just number.
TOW: You will die soon enough, old man!
FATHER M: So why commit a mortal sin and condemn my soul to
        everlasting flames?
        Why make this pathetic gesture?
        Why set this bad example?

Seats himself at the table.

        Is it too much to ask for a death of my own?

TOW: Too much! Way too much!

FATHER M: That was supposed to be a rhetorical question!
Is it too much even to have a moment of my own
To think of that moment.
To think of that moment when I might
Touch life to death by their very edges?
Life with still a little quiver left in it;
Death taken just a little by surprise.
A mating. A begetting.
A begetting, a begetting.
Is it too much to ask for a death of my own?

Sound, faint at first, of tolling bells. The sound will increase and become more complex with overlapping resonations as he continues to reflect.

I must finish my lists!
Thirdly—Against. No, make that, Thirdly—For.

A moment of helplessness, then a new resolve. He will now speak in a more adult, measured, and authoritative voice.

Enough!

Seizes and crumples up both sheets of paper. Rises.

TOW: Father Muncrief!
FATHER M: Enough!

It is now becoming difficult to hear him because of the increasing volume of the tolling heads. He is continuing to speak, arguing with himself in a kind of rapture. We hear only a few words that escape the growing din, but see him in a rapid birdlike alternation of posture, pointing fingers back and forth at his contrarian self. Each self has a characteristic voice and tone.

. . . Mortal	Love . . .
. . . Taste	Death . . .
. . . Hold	The night . . .
. . . The reason For	
. . . Hold	The night . . .

Final crescendo.

Blackout

NOTEBOOK

Suicide is never just about suicide. It is about belief, doubt, hurt, and disappointment. It is about the implicit contract that a person assumes has been made with society and the universe—and how one responds when this contract seems to have been violated or cancelled. Suicide is about life—and, sometimes, only incidentally about death.

In experiencing these few minutes with Father Muncrief we see a man who is determined to be rational in reaching his decision. Whether he will or will not take his life may seem almost secondary to making the decision in the "right" way. He must justify his decision—but to whom? To God? To himself? To the tart voices of his past? Or to us, the witnesses of today and the custodians of the future?

Somehow Father Muncrief has come to the point where faith in logic is being called upon to accomplish what faith in faith did not. His logic is also strained, however. Again, questions rise more easily than answers: just how rational is it to rely so confidently on rationality? And why does his available past speak to him only with reproaches and regrets? Where are the voices of appreciation and approbation? Did he set the wrong course for his life, or did he follow stars that were themselves errant? Is it even thinkable to us that suicide perhaps might be the most rational choice for some people in some situations?

There will be a strong temptation for audiences to place value judgements on the character of Father Muncrief and his consideration of suicide. All the available stereotypes that brand suicide as the act of a weak, inept, disordered, or sinful person are likely to express themselves. There will also be a strong tendency to become exercised about the For/Against decision. An insightful performance and a skillful follow-up discussion can succeed in redirecting attention to Father Muncrief himself (and any and every old man on the verge of suicide). To be sure, suicidal crisis demands attention. This attention, however, must also surely encompass an individual's total life quest and struggle within the context of particular interpersonal relationships and particular cultural values, contradictions, and pressures. In other words: we don't know much about Father Muncrief's possible suicide unless we have educated ourselves about the man and his times.

Father Muncrief's List can provide a beneficially disquieting supplement to conferences and classes that are considering the challenging topic of elderly suicide. It is also suitable for disrupting otherwise coherent educational programs in the broader area of social gerontology, as well as counseling, family development, and religious studies.

A gifted actor can offer an effective reading of *Father Muncrief's List* sans the opening visuals. Invest the effort, however, in providing Ella's song and a hearty set of recorded bells. (The Ella Fitzgerald number can be found on Verve CD 0383: The Irving Berlin Songbook, Volume 2, and in several other incarnations. Bell-wise, there are several good choices to be found on a CD entitled Glocken in Russland (Bells in Russia), Christophorous 74553. Several other labels provide bell samplers on sound effect CDs. But feel free to substitute your own local vocalist for Ella (providing she can produce that smoky swing), or to record from your own friendly neighborhood belfry. Similarly, if you can't come up with Bach's Gigue from Partita No. 6, substitute another keyboard piece that is both animated and logically relentless.

But should you perform this play in the first place? Here's how to decide: Draw up two lists . . . and call me in the morning.

Vienna, City of My Dreams

TIME AND PLACE: *Vienna, 1938. SIGMUND FREUD's consulting room in his apartment at 19 Bergasse. Furnished in comfortable, somewhat ornate style. Near the famous couch is his desk with its collection of figurines from many tribal cultures. Book cases in the background. The 82-year-old physician, wearing his customary conservative suit, is sitting in a straight chair at the head of the couch. We will hear various people, but see only Freud.*

AT RISE: *Offstage distant sound of crowd at mass demonstration. Lights gradually rise. We see Freud perched intently on the chair, his elbows flared back, listening to the demonstration. He seems on the verge of rising for combat. Crowd noise heightens.*

MILITANT VOICE: Against the soul-destroying glorification of the instinctual life, for the nobility of the human soul! I consign to the flames the writings of the school of Sigmund Freud! [*Crowd uproar, slowly fading*]

FREUD: Today it seems I am an artist's model. The young man in the next room is occupied in transforming me into a statue. I am to become an immortal while my books curl into smoke. I do not require the sculptor's assistance. Life hardens me continuously. The sour-faced statues at the University could take lessons from me. I suppose they would be envious. "Who is that grim old gargoyle? Even the pigeons fear to roost on him!" "Why that's a Doctor Freud of 19 Bergasse." "God save the Emperor—there goes our neighborhood!"

[*Relaxing a moment from the uncomfortable modeling position*]

I did not speak to young Mr. Nemon for a week. Not a word. One day I surprised him. "Did you know that your profession is the oldest in the world?" He had no reply— I like that in a young man! "Yes, it is true: did not God create man from clay?" This may be the primal joke, so we should not expect it to be very funny. And the joke, of course, is on us. [*In quiet intensity*] My clay has grown cold with age and hard with anger. I condense. I crack.

And still I am asked to pose, either in person or on the printed page. This morning I was asked to write an article for a special issue of a magazine that will concern itself with the persecution of the Jews. With the new persecution of the Jews, that is. Or, rather, with the continued persecution.

[*Rises, stretches a little. Closes the window. Withdraws a small notebook from inside jacket pocket from which he will read the letter*]

I could write only a single paragraph [*reads*]
"Dear Sir:
I came to Vienna as a child of four years from a small town in Moravia. After 78 years I have to leave my home, see the scientific society I founded dissolved, our printing press taken over by the invaders, my books confiscated and reduced to pulp and smoke, my children ousted from their professions. Don't you think the columns of your special number might rather be reserved for the utterance of non-Jewish people less personally involved than myself?
Yours, Freud."

Oh! [*Reacts to the unseen Nemon returning to the study*]. Yes, yes. Back to the immortality business. [*Assumes his previous position.*] Just for another little moment? Tell me a new one! What I would give for a cigar. Forbidden of course. What? Have you really finished—at last? [*Arises. Inspects the unseen statue beyond the audience's line of vision. Offers a nod of grudging approval.*] I am glad you put in enough anger! [*A benign gesture to the departing sculptor.*]

Perhaps I am free now from this monstrosity, this heavy monumentality so beloved of the Viennese. May Nemon's statue replace me in the public gaze. How inconvenient that one cannot replace those other monstrosities—the withering flesh and the arrogant mind.
[*Crosses to his desk. Selects and fondles one of the figurines before settling himself in the more comfortable chair behind the desk.*]

There are ways, of course. One can impersonate the Great Reaper and slay the grass of one's own flesh before it perishes in season. But who does one truly slay? Self murder often kills the inner representation of one we have most desperately loved. World—I have desperately loved you—in my own grim way, of course. Would I murder myself to ease my agony and destroy the you in me? Not on my life! All-Promising World, All-Deceiving World—I will not let you off so easy!

[*Referring to the figurine.*] This charming figurine is an ancient god who presided over intoxication, much like Bacchus. That is still another way out. I could drug this incessant, this insatiable, this arrogant mind that has seldom allowed me a moment's rest. I could rid myself and the world of this unpopular observer.

But here I am, still. Seven causes of death are competing for the doubtful honor of ending my days. The agony from my throat cancer I would not wish on anybody and, yet to think, I wished it on myself! What I would give for a cigar. And still this arrogant mind will not give Doctor Schur the satisfaction of accepting his morphine. I wish I could put him out of my misery.

There. Back to your brothers and sisters in mythology.
[*Replacing the figurine.*] Even before the Nazis, I felt more

comfortable with these honest demons than with the good people of Vienna. What hidden god do they worship? And does it really demand daily offerings of whipped cream and hypocrisy?

By all that is right and holy, it is time to return to the womb of time. Ah, I suppose I am terribly slow in taking the hint. I have just come through some particularly unpleasant weeks. Four months ago I had one of my normal operations. This was followed by unusually violent pain. I had to cancel my work for twelve days. Twelve days! I lay uselessly with pain and hot-water bottles on the couch which is meant for others.

Scarcely had I resumed work when world history brewed in a tea cup and changed all our lives forever. On the wireless I listened first to our proud Austrian challenge and then to our surrender—to the rejoicing and the counter-rejoicing. Our dusty old Empire has given itself to Hitler in the blink of an eye.

Sound: Woman's voice lightly laughing. A sophisticated French-accented woman in her 20's or 30's

FREUD: Do I know that laugh? There has not been much to find amusing here lately. I am not yet quite free from pain. The last of my few patients have left me. I do absolutely nothing.

MADAME D: What sport! To meet at last the founder of psychoanalysis! To find out at last why it is that when one dreams of dead elderducks it means that one has a libinal desire for one's maternal grandmother—what joy! What intoxication!

FREUD: Madame DuBois! There can be no doubt! The patient I saw only last week after I had made it perfectly clear I was too old and sick to be of any earthly help to anybody. But she persuaded others to persuade me that I was the only person who could help her. In my weakness, I consented.

MADAME D: Everything is dirty, everything! What is clean is dirty and what is dirty is disgusting, and everything is disgusting! I must wash myself continuously, and that is so tiring. A hundred times a day I wash. I moisten and soap and scrub and rinse every inch of my body. The trouble is that the minute one is through, one must begin all over again, because one is always dirty. It is SO tiring!

FREUD: She also claimed to be terrified of dogs. Apparently she was an irresistible morsel to all canines. And there were other enchanting features to her case as well. Even now, I am vulnerable to the interesting case.

MADAME D: [*Speaking now in her normal journalistic voice*]
Freud is 82 years old, but looks only sixty. Beautiful hair. Well combed and brushed. A short beard. His eyes have retreated behind his spectacles. You feel they are burning into you every moment. His hands are strangely young, and there is still so much youth in the way he speaks and moves.

FREUD: I did not know that she was a journalist masquerading as a neurotic. Or is it a masquerade? What is today's journalist but a voyeuristic child who continues to spy on Momma and Pappa through the key hole? Forget I said that! I have stirred up enough trouble already! This is how I "treated" the spectacularly neurotic Madame DuBois: Madame DuBois? *Sprechen sie Deutsche? Nein?* Well, then, how do you expect me to practice psychoanalysis with you? Doubtless you speak only French! I knew that slippery language once, but such a long time ago. I am old. I have forgotten everything!

MADAME D: Perhaps we can speak English together.

FREUD: Bless my old ears! Are you speaking English now? But if you do not speak louder, there is not the slightest use beginning any treatment. I am a little bit deaf—it is my age. I cannot understand a word. Can't you raise your voice?

MADAME D: Certainly, Dr. Freud. Can you hear me now?

FREUD: So faintly.

MADAME D: CAN YOU HEAR ME NOW?

FREUD: Aha! You do not sound like a depressed person, Madame DuBois! You are not a depressed person, Madame DuBois!

MADAME D: BUT SURELY I AM DEPRESSED—I INSIST ON BEING DEPRESSED

FREUD: You see, Madame DuBois, it is easy to assume a stricken air when one speaks low. But let the voice be raised and instantly the eyes clear, the brow smooths, color returns into your cheeks, and there is nothing left of depression and distress. A cure in less than a minute! And people say that psychoanalysis takes years!

MADAME D: I am not cured all the way down to my toes!

FREUD: One more moment and you will be an appallingly joyful creature. I am going to show you how you cannot help but be happy.

MADAME D: Is such a thing possible?

FREUD: Do just as I say. First: watch me. [*FREUD smiles.*] Now you do that.

MADAME D: Do what?

FREUD: That! Oh, don't make me smile again; I have no need to be happy. But—watch closely. [*A deliberately therapeutic smile.*]
          Not bad! But not good. You can do better, of that I am certain. Again: this time smile along with me. Are you ready? One . . . two . . . three, smile! Ah, that was more like it! Once again now—smile the merriest and most glorious smile in all of creation—[*FREUD gives us his very best smile, too*]—there!

          You are charming now, Madame DuBois, absolutely charming. Why don't you always want to smile? How can you keep your absolutely charming self from smiling and beautifying the world for all who behold you?
          She never came back, of course.

MADAME D: I never came back, of course. It was more than enough to meet the great Professor Freud! Ten thousand other reporters envy me. I even envy myself!

FREUD: She did have a charming smile. One of my more spectacular cures! But then it is simple to cure conditions that do not exist. I suppose she will tell the world that she pulled one over on old Freud. Ah, well, I can't cure that!

MADAME D: He said . . . I had a charming smile . . .

FREUD: And she looked at me then . . . the way . . . a woman looks at a man! So! That was good for a smile! No small blessing,

these days. Rest is also a blessing. What little rest I can coax from this old cracked stone of a body.
[*Rises, crosses to the couch, adjusts a pillow*]

This couch is not a resting place. It is the most rest-less couch in Vienna. I am certain it has absorbed legions of fantasies and fears from some of the most talented neurotics of five continents. One's brain could be eaten alive by them. But I must take this risk for a moment. [*Lies down*] The body demands sleep. But dreams? No comfort there, not for me. The fulfillment of wishes, the making of wrong things right? The dream is not my haven; it is my workplace. Even if I wanted to be the sentimental old man listening to dream voices, I could not bring myself to take my eye off the world. It must be the same with Einstein. And have you seen the sky tonight? Have you ever seen such blood written upon the heavens? Ah . . .
[*FREUD settles into sleep*]

Blackout

Music: Recording of "Vienna, City of My Dreams," sung by suitably Viennese tenor or soprano. After a minute . . .

Lighting change: suggesting a fresh and promising morning

FREUD rises from the couch, energetic, sprightly, apparently in midlife vigor.

FREUD:　　　Welcome, dear friends, to Vienna! I am the least Viennese person in this city, but who does not respond to the music, the pride, the lure of Vienna! Did you recognize the song? It has become inescapable lately: "Vienna, City of My Dreams!" Obviously this was the perfect city in which to develop my interpretation of dreams. [*Selects, admires, ignites and enjoys a cigar as he goes along*]
I excavate dreams the way that Schliemann excavated the ancient city of Troy. He gave us the gift of our collective

past. I offer the rediscovery of our own very selves. He dug for treasure in places others considered barren. Myself likewise: in the slip of the tongue, the choice of a word, the symbolic connections between one action and another. And, best of all, in the dream.

Troy and Vienna . . . Vienna and Troy. To me, the ancient city of Troy feels more solid than this golden, glittering Vienna that tenors and soprano's cannot stop warbling about. But you must see Vienna and judge for yourself. Can I interest you in a stroll? [*Equips himself with hat and umbrella.*]

Sound: Dog barks hopefully.

Yes, Wolf, you can come, too!

FREUD moves through the available performance space. Lighting changes demarcate the venues as they are visited. This scene can either be accompanied by visuals or left to the imagination as tutored by FREUD's observations.

Do you have an eye for architecture? Here you would need a thousand eyes! Monumental buildings pose for us on every side. What's that, you say? Yes, I must agree. Vienna does have an "Edifice Complex." I must remember that one!

This specimen? The Rathaus. A harrowing neo-Gothic. And there? That is the Palace of Justice. Neo-Renaissance. Also neo-Italian Mannerism. And who knows neo what else! *Helas!* And here we have neo-Greek! You are starting to grasp the stylistic principle, I am sure. Neo-anything. Neo-everything.

Indeed, it is all quite impressive at first sight. Only after some years have I been able to see Vienna for what it is. These emblems of imperial glory are not solid entities. They are all but reflections in a mirror, reflections cleverly arranged to reflect the triumphs of long vanished civilizations and proclaim these as our own.

Optional: Visual effect transforming a handsome ancient structure into an exaggerated, distorted, menacing edifice.

But the mirror is distorted. We do not see the purity of the Greeks or the exuberance of the baroque. Balance is lost. Ornaments pile on ornaments. Bad taste elevates into a principle and perhaps even into a reason for being. My friends, if it can be stolen, distorted, and exaggerated, you will find it here in Vienna.

Lighting change

Oh, my apologies! I did not mean to expose you to this part of Vienna! Wolf must have lead us astray—wicked dog! We will exit this area immediately, and forget about it even sooner. That is the Viennese way!

The City of Dreams could not be littered by the unemployed, the drunken, and the perverse, therefore it is not. Those adolescent girls looked to you like under-nourished and diseased prostitutes? Forgive me, but that observation only reveals how little you know of magical Vienna. They are princesses, princesses all, and only a bit weary after waltzing all night at the palace.

Lighting change

Good! We are back to official tour book Vienna. More monuments to our glory. The Museum of Natural History. Excellent. And it really does have two staircases, one for going up, one for going down! A little joke here.

That lovely park? It's a theater. True! We call it Central Cemetery. A stage set, actually, where glory becomes stone and stone becomes glory. The Viennese do funerals very well. Naturally, they—we—insist on a quality stage setting.

Music: Passage from Schubert's C major Quintet, Op. 163, Adagio movement.

Many of the great composers have been installed here. And, frankly, it is the first peace and respect they have known in Vienna. [*FREUD doffs his hat and listens in silence for a moment.*]

Music ends

And so I have given you Vienna! But I have given you nothing! A city of facades, a city of dreams. More precisely: a city of dreamers. The dream-work of wish-fulfillment! You have seen it petrified and you have heard it flow in three-quarter time. Petrified or flowing, it is not reason or achievement that Vienna enjoys, but only an ornamental slumber.
[*FREUD and his invisible entourage have now circled back to his study. He puts his cigar in an ash tray, and sits at the edge of the couch.*]

Vienna is not the city of my dreams. On the contrary. The self-deceit, the emptiness, the terror beneath the facade in this city keep me awake at night. Others it has driven to suicide. Some of our best!
[*Appearing progressively older and more fatigued*]

Look all you please at our facades. Dance all you please to our Schmaltz. But—if I may speak as a friend—do not penetrate beyond the facade nor ask the fiddler's price unless you are as persistent as a Schliemann and as unblinking as a Freud.
[*Lies down, letting the umbrella slip from his hand and without thinking to remove his hat.*]

Blackout

VOICE: (EINSTEIN) [*Optional: slide projection: ALBERT EINSTEIN*]
Dear Professor Freud:
I feel elated that the League of Nations has given me the unique opportunity to discuss with you those questions which in the present state of world affairs appear to me to be the most important ones facing civilization.
Is there a way to liberate mankind from the doom of war? How is it possible that the mass of the people permits itself to become aroused to the point of insanity and eventual self-sacrifice by these means?
The answer can only be . . .

Lights rise: midnight ambience. FREUD—old and pained—suddenly stirs from his sleep and completes the sentence

FREUD: The answer can only be: man has in him the need to hate and to destroy.
[*He is not completely awake. Takes a moment to orient himself, arises slowly, finds his reading glasses, is puzzled also to find the hat on his head and the umbrella on the floor.*]

Did I dream again of Wolf? What a hole was left in our lives! But it is Einstein's letter that disturbs me now as it has for weeks. What am I to reply with the world looking over our shoulders?
[*Crosses to his desk, picks up the Einstein letter; it falls from his hand. He stoops to retrieve it, but instead goes to his knees runs his hand across the floor in an exploratory way.*]
Roses and blood . . . life sinking into death and life rising out of death. One can feel it, smell it, taste it through the floor, through the walls, through all that divides us from nature. Perhaps I should not be writing a letter with answers. Perhaps I should be confessing my questions directly into Mother's ear.
[*Settles more comfortably on the floor—stiff with age, but in easy communion with Nature. In just above a whisper . . .*]

"Dear Earth, Dear Mother:
Madam—I cannot explain why we rush so swiftly into your dark embrace. Yet, why roses these days exhale the stench of blood is not so difficult to explain. I should not be surprised if tomorrow's roses will have become carnivorous! We are killers, dear Madam.

Lighting: Gradually taking on a red tinge

Civilization is our greatest achievement. And yet, the civilized Germans and the civilized English and the civilized Russians—and even the half-civilized Americans—we have all of us not lost our taste for blood. To the contrary, we have become insatiable.

And now we are teaching the flowers! I myself no longer trust the butterfly or the rainbow. This very morning I heard a mortar shell discharged by a small brown toad, and the birds nesting on my roof twitter like a battery of machine guns.

Do you suppose we have perhaps all gone just a little too far?

Your sweet and obedient child—Freud.
[*Rising with the letter*]

No! Let me sign that instead: Carl C. Jung. Of Zurich! He always likes to let on that he has a very special relationship with Mother!

Perhaps—perhaps I must speak also with Father. But which Father? The old man who snored beside my mother and had so few words for me? Our Father Which Art Raging in an Old Testament whirlwind? Or enthroned in a New Testament paradise? My Fatherland who crushes his own children with iron jackboots? Or myself, a father- figure to some and a target to not a few?

Father—where are you? [*Listens: nothing*]

Father—I do not have much time left. As a very old man, Jacob was taken by his children to Egypt. In a few days I must also leave my home land forever—but was it ever home?
Father—how will I find the strength to live and die in England while the flames of madness rise all about us like a hideous opera by Wagner?

Father—how should I speak to you?

Sound and light: Impressive rolling thunder having the effect of a cosmic fanfare. Lightning flashes.

[*FREUD is apprehensive but impressed*]
FREUD: Father?

Storm fades. The voice heard next is that of a hesitant, unpretentious male with a rich Jewish accent

THE JEW: It is just me. Sorry about the thunder and lightning.
FREUD: Sorry?
THE JEW: I don't do the thunder and lightning around here. It just follows me around.
FREUD: Are you Father? Are you God? Or just a bad dream?
THE JEW: With the last one, you are getting close. In a word: I am The Jew.
FREUD: The Jew. Yes, it's coming back to me. Where have you been all these years? And what will become of you now?
THE JEW: I am not so good at answers, Professor.
FREUD: "Professor." He pronounces the word as though it were a sweet melon on his tongue. Of course, how could I have forgotten. The Jew starves after learning, while those who sit around the table pick at the meal with so little appetite.
THE JEW: Professor, it is only me. It is only the Jew, the outcast, the wandering one. I thought, well, I hoped that just perhaps . . .
FREUD: Yes, go on. You thought what? Just perhaps what?

THE JEW:	Can we perhaps walk the rest of the way together?
FREUD:	It is I who must ask permission to walk along with you.
THE JEW:	Professor, an honor. So: where are we going?
FREUD:	I thought you knew!
THE JEW:	What I know is how to place one foot in front of the other and keep moving.
	[*FREUD is walking comfortably as with a companion on a long hike*]
FREUD:	Through the thunder.
THE JEW:	Of course, through the thunder.
FREUD:	Through the lightning.
THE JEW:	Of course, through the lightning.
FREUD:	Knowing what answers?
THE JEW:	Knowing—some good questions!
FREUD:	Einstein asked me some good questions.
THE JEW:	So I heard. I have a good one for you myself.
	[*FREUD stops to fetch his umbrella and hat before continuing his trek in earnest*]
FREUD:	What is your good question?
THE JEW:	Do you hate me? Do you want to kill me? Actually, two questions. Choose either one.
FREUD:	Same answer for both. Of course, I don't hate you and of course I don't want to kill you.
THE JEW:	Ah . . . for a while there, you could have fooled me!
FREUD:	It was Freud I was fooling. I like Freud better now that we have become companions again.
THE JEW:	So why not tell Einstein and the League of Nations?
FREUD:	Why not? [*Writing in his notebook*] I agree with you that the destructive side of human nature is real. It cannot be wished away. How can we control this enemy within? By calling upon the other side. *Eros!* Aggression is real but the same may be said for love. This equally profound sentiment is also rooted in our being. Psychoanalysis need not be ashamed when it speaks of love.
THE JEW:	Now, that's my Professor!
FREUD:	Anything that creates emotional ties between human beings must surely counteract war. *We must love ourself in the other person, and the other person in ourself.* As simple as that! As difficult as that!

THE JEW: You look better!
FREUD: I feel better! I am ready to complete another disagreeable essay. This one will be on "Moses and Monotheism."
THE JEW: Monotheism? One God—that was for Moses enough!
FREUD: That was sometimes for me—too many!

Thunder and lightning reprise

THE JEW: Professor, they're playing our song!
FREUD: [*Opens umbrella*] Come friend. There's room for you here. There's room for everybody here.

Offstage: Barking dog:

              You too, Wolf! Come wicked dog!
              [*FREUD starts to exit slowly, umbrella held high*]

Loudest thunder, brightest streak of lightning—
then Blackout

NOTEBOOK

The unfinished business of our private lives tends to press its demands "as the days dwindle down to a precious few." This quirk of our mental-emotional apparatus has been recognized by Erik Erikson in his final epigenetic stage (Integrity vs. Despair), by Robert Butler in his life review theory, and by numerous authors and diarists. Indeed, in composing his classic "September Song," Kurt Weil was well aware of the irony: his own name could be translated as "Short Time."

Vienna, City of My Dreams introduces us into the private world of another creative person who, like Weil and many other gifted artists, scientists, and physicians, fled from Vienna one step ahead of "the final solution." Sigmund Freud's private world, however, had long become universal property. He had descended into the uncharted territory of his own "unconscious," to emerge with the most controversial gift since Pandora's box: psychoanalytic theory. As the once-obscure fortyish physician grew old he heard his work both praised and damned extravagantly throughout the world. Freud's conflicts were now everybody's conflicts. Even his staunchest foes used Freudian concepts and techniques in attempts to discredit him.

Devoting much of one's life to exploring the depths of private experience, however, does not provide insulation from the tides of misfortune and catastrophe that threaten to engulf civilization. Although he harbored fewer illusions than other men, Freud was shaken by the explosion of violence that characterized The Great War and by the parallel rise in suicide and mean-spiritedness in the wake of his nation's defeat. We join him in his 82nd year, a fragile and agonized man who fears for the future of civilization more than for his own impending death.

Old Man Freud provides a rare opportunity to explore the challenge of completing one's own unfinished business while caught up in a business that threatened to finish all of us. He is burdened with being considered "the expert" at the same time that he is facing a grim matter for the first time himself—the apparent triumph of brutality. How is he to deal with the forces of destruction that are on the street around him and, soon, at his door? That is to say, how is he to deal with these forces as a "doctor to the soul" and a philosopher of human experience, as well as a terminally ill old man?

Freud was not a wild-eyed, radical, diabolic character and should not be played as such. Let him be the precise, cautious, responsible, stubborn, and somewhat "held-in" person that emerges from his letters and from the testimony of many who knew him well. His flashes of humor and spontaneity are real enough, but should appear like shafts of unexpected sunlight on a foreboding day. The anger should also show through—more as a laser beam emanating from a powerful and controlled source than as a capricious outburst.

His basic orientation to the audience is marked by his inspectorial gaze: appraising, uncompromising, don't-think-for-a-moment-you-can-fool-me. In fact, he does quite a bit of intense looking and listening, within which his own words emerge—he is not just talking at people all of the time. A talented Freud will not allow the audience to become too comfortable with him. And yet his approach is not hostile. Guarded, not easily persuaded, more than a little skeptical—but not hostile. When the occasion permits, he can be very warm and charming indeed. His usually precise and somewhat stiff manner of speech becomes more animated and feelingful at certain moments.

At one level, *Vienna, City of My Dreams* samples one old man's coming-to-terms with his unique life in its unique times. At another level, it is a more universal encounter between the courage to see and call things as they are and the ever-present temptations of hypocrisy and retreat. Perhaps most simply, it is an experiment to determine whether love is possible for this so-often impossible human race.

Script-in-hand presentation can be effective with a talented Freud, adequate rehearsal, and utilization of sound and lighting effects. Consider going all the way, though: a full production does not require that much more. (The song that is known in English as "Vienna, City of My Dreams" can be difficult to locate on record these days. Perhaps the most readily available is a cream-smooth version by Fritz Wunderlich in a memorial collection on three boxed Deutsche Grammaphon CDs, #435-145-2. It is listed under its German title which does not actually refer to dreams: "Wien, Wien, Nur Du Allein." Several grittier older performances would be more in keeping with the play if they can be found. Skip the intro and start play with the romantic old tune. Or perhaps your circle of friends happens to include a singer with a legitimate voice who remembers this once very popular song from his/her own youth?)

(The present version is a condensation and synthesis of the full-length script, *Doctor Freud Will See You Now!*)

The Girl in the Raindrop

Characters

VALERIE: *13-year-old girl with a life-threatening disease (leukemia). In reality, she is hospitalized and receiving treatment in a special-precautions isolation room. In fantasy, she is most everywhere.*

SNUFFY: *Valerie's deceased dog. Now only a ghostly woof.*

THANATRIC I: *A poster-carrying scene-setter who also takes various auxiliary roles, becoming increasingly involved in the action.*

BIKEMAN: *A merry, grandiose and virile man of the 1890s—but also more than that. He also appears, in another of his guises, as* Thanatric III.

ATROPES: *One of the classic Fates, here taking the form of a blue follow spot.*

DR. STERN: *Valerie's physician (Voice only).*

BROTHER (Valerie's): *Typical worthless kid brother. Seen once, but not heard.*

MOM (Valerie's): *A normal person faced with abnormal stress.*

DAD (Valerie's): *The same may be said about him.*

NURSE: *All she gets to do is carry in a tray and smile. We'll have to make this up to her in the sequel.*

THANATRIC II: *Colleague of Than I.*

THANATRIC III: *Who in Labyrinth II is* Bird-than *and dances his way into our hearts (or, maybe not).*

BIBLE LADY: *An assertive yet endearing personage who stops just short of caricature.*

THE BIG GUY: *Voice only.*

REALITY MAN: *A fine specimen of the establishment type. At last, somebody who makes sense!*

Scenes

WE ARE ALL IN THE DARK, (*Prologue*)
DAISY DOES IT
LITTLE PINK GLOVES, (*Labyrinth I*)
THE BIBLE LADY BLUES
WHATSOEVER, (*Labyrinth II*)
PROCEED AT YOUR OWN RISK
PLACES TO GO, (*Finale*)

We Are All in the Dark (Prologue)

Character: VALERIE, whose expressive little voice with its frequent shifts in pitch and intonation is heard (from a ceiling speaker if possible), although she is not yet seen.

Blackout

Ooooh! Weird! I need some weird music, please!

Weird music begins

Thank you! Here I am and there I am. Me and me. Me down there and me up here. *Look* at that Down There Me! What a stupid little snot! She can't do a thing. Hey, Me! Has your brain turned to jello? Can you hear me! You are one pitiful sight. Do yourself a favor—get buried! Ooooh! That's not nice for me to say to me. [*In "Tonto" accent*] Me say me one heap bad hombre. What you say, Masked Man? Ah! Wooo-ooh! I feel *so* good! It's great being the Me Up Here. I just think of something and I can do it. I'm floating on the ceiling! I'm dancing on the clouds! I'm an angel! Oh, I'm so sweet! Don't kiss me—you might catch diabetes! [*She sings along with the music for a moment*].

Music ends

Now I think it's time. Time to meet a spirit. That's what's supposed to happen, you know. A *ra-diant* spirit. Spirit, spirit in the air. Come on out, I know you're there!

Sound from distant source:

WOOF! WOOF! WOOF!

Snuffy! Is that *you?* You're not a spirit! You're a dog!

WOOF!

All right—you're a dog and a spirit. A spirit-dog! Snuffy—is this where you went when you went away? Did they send me to Doggy Heaven by mistake? Come here, silly dog!

Dog pantings and squeals

You silly dog! Do you get your Pupperoni's up here? Do they even *have* trees? Tell me, Wise Old Spirit: Am I dead already, or just practicing? I don't like it Down There any more. I want to come with *you.* I want to *be* with you. OK, Snuffy? Snuffy!

Agitated music

Lighting change: Rapidly changing chaotic flashes, zaps, and blips. Disorienting effect [strobe on THANATRICS in disorganized motion.] Then: Silence and blackout. Slide projections of the following titles

(1) The Girl in the Raindrop
(2) (That's me)
(3) A Pretty Desperate Production
(4) Starring Me, Valerie
(5) With Special Guest Appearances by all Sorts of People and Things and Even a Dog
(6) Though You Don't Actually Get to See the Dog
(7) Well, That's all the Slides I Have for Now
(8) Prologue: We Are All in The Dark

Oh, I forgot that one. I've already done it. But I think we should call it instead:

(9) A Near-Life Experience

I'm *near* to life. But it doesn't really feel like life. Not like much of a life, anyhow. So I make up a lot of stuff. I put some of it into this play. Hope you like it.

(10) Now The Play is *Really* Starting!

Stage lights gradually rise

Daisy Does It

Characters:

THANATRIC, BIKEMAN, DR. STERN [voice]

Lighting: Bright, sunny. Bed and bedside table upstage far right for all scenes. Offstage right: Somebody [BIKEMAN] is whistling "Daisy." From offstage left, THAN crosses briskly, holding the post. Has almost exited right when he remembers he has not shown the poster. Embarrassed, returns to center stage, and displays the bright yellow poster: DAISY DOES IT.

At this moment, BIKEMAN rides on from offstage right on his old-fashioned contraption. He is dressed colorfully with polo shirt, knickers, high yellow socks, and gaudy yellow scarf. He also sports an outrageously exaggerated handlebar moustache spreading out under his nose like a majestic tree. BIKEMAN wears a dazzling sunny smile of well-being that he shines on the audience. He merrily rides a circle around the stage, whistling "Daisy" as he goes. Comes to a flashy stop—a wheelie would be grand—dismounts by the bike and strikes a much-pleased-with-myself stance

BIKEMAN: *[To audience, with dominatingly exuberant charm]* You know this song! It's everybody's favorite! Sing along with me—sing along—I'll give you the words:

Daisy, Daisy
[*Conducts audience in singing this phrase*]
Give me your answer true
[*Will continue to conduct the audience*]
I'm half crazy
[*Audience response*]
All for the love of you
[*Audience response*]

VALERIE enters from left. She wears a straw bonnet with a yellow ribbon and carries a pretty little parasol that she twirls with indolent pleasure as she first takes in the scene, and then strolls in a slow, ladylike, but also slightly predatory manner.

BIKEMAN: [*Continuing, at first he does not notice VALERIE*]
I can't afford a carriage
[*Audience response*]
Or a stylish marriage
[*Audience response*]

He notices VALERIE and addresses the rest of the lyrics to her.

But you'd look sweet
[*Audience response*]
Upon the seat
[*Audience response*]
Of a bicycle built for two!
[*Audience response*]

BIKEMAN applauds audience. VALERIE strolls closer, pridefully in control of situation. She inspects him, then also briefly appraises audience with a nod and a dismissive shrug of her shoulders. BIKEMAN is hopeful.

BIKEMAN: Lovely day, Ma'am.
VALERIE: It will do, I suppose [*She is playing with him.*]
BIKEMAN: Lovely day for birds! [*Imitates a bird call or two.*]
Lovely day for ducks! [*Quacks and mimes a duck.*]
Even a lovely day for frogs [*Croaks and mimes.*]

VALERIE: [*Amused*] You are a one-man landscape—or is that, swampscape! I would say your talent resides less in tweeting than in croaking.

BIKEMAN: It is an honor to amuse so lovely a lady.

VALERIE: Oh yes, I should say so! What else do you do?

BIKEMAN: Do you mean impersonations?

VALERIE: Or impertinations!

She is circling slowly about him, tantalizingly aware of her charms though, of course, still completely the lady

BIKEMAN: I do palpitations! Perturbations! Imprecations! Adumbrations! Tin-tin-tab-u-lations!

VALERIE: All that? How droll. And how dull.

BIKEMAN: Wait! For ladies of refinement, I do much more. Actually, my talents are unlimited.

VALERIE: [*Running her fingers sensuously along the handlebar*] Give a man a bicycle and he thinks himself the very devil!

BIKEMAN: This is not just any bicycle, ma'am. Come. A little ride. You will see for yourself.

VALERIE: [*Feigned anger*] Do I seem like that type of woman? The common sort who accept rides from any young scamp who happens along?

BIKEMAN: You seem—indeed you *are*—the most *un*common. The fairest, the rarest. The flower of flowers.

VALERIE: They call me, Daisy

BIKEMAN: The daisy of daisies.

VALERIE: But, you see, it is quite impossible.

BIKEMAN: Impossible?

VALERIE: I simply cannot abide men with hair crawling over their faces.

BIKEMAN: For you, Daisy, nothing is impossible. [*He tears off the moustache*]

VALERIE: But a *handlebar* moustache! That is entirely different! I *adore* handlebar moustaches!

BIKEMAN: My pleasure, ma'am [*He attaches the moustache to the bike's handlebars*]

VALERIE: [*Clapping her hands in delight.*] You win!

She playfully scruffles the moustache, and seats herself on the handlebar as BIKEMAN steadies the bike and then takes his seat.

BIKEMAN: Where to, ma'am?
VALERIE: Daisy! You may call me, Daisy. I would go, oh, somewhere
           else! Somewhere I have never, ever been!
BIKEMAN: Perfect, Daisy! Precisely the destination I had in mind!

BIKEMAN whistles "Daisy" as they ride across the stage, and exit left, with VALERIE holding on to both her bonnet and parasol.

VALERIE: Oooh! The Taj Mahal! I've seen a picture of it! India!

They reenter immediately and navigate most of the stage in the longest, slowest possible arc.

VALERIE: Buckminster Palace! [*Waving*] Queen! Yoo-hoo! It's
           Daisy! Sorry, I can't stop for tea.... The Eiffel Tower! Has
           it stopped leaning? Oh, that's the wrong tower! The Great
           Wall of China! My, how it does go on! Keep pedaling,
           Bikeman, keep pedaling!
BIKEMAN: As you wish, Daisy
VALERIE: Stop! [*He does*] I feel a salty breeze. I can hear the breakers.
           What ocean is it, what sea?
BIKEMAN: Which one would you like? The Caspian Sea? The Black
           Sea? The Dead Sea?
VALERIE: No, not that! A *nice* kind of sea. Or, better, a whole
           ocean.
BIKEMAN: What do you think of this one? [*He helps her dismount,
           then leads her, with a light touch, to lip of stage.*]
VALERIE: Oh, it's heavenly. The rocks. The beach. The tide advanc-
           ing and retreating. The foam splashing and glistening. The
           sun glowing as it sinks on the horizon. My, it must be
           getting late!
BIKEMAN: Does that trouble you?
VALERIE: [*Troubled*] No! I can do as I choose. I have all the time I
           want. I have all the time in the world.
BIKEMAN: As you say, Daisy, as you wish.
VALERIE: As I wish . . . I wish I were a fish.

BIKEMAN: [*Laughing*] A fish? I have seen a star fish! But a daisy fish? But—why not!

VALERIE: I wish I were a fish. Hidden in the deep. I wish I were a fish hidden in the deep blue sea.

Lighting change: Blue spot for her

BIKEMAN: [*Displaying her*] Behold the daisy fish. Queen of the deep blue sea. An extraordinary specimen. But why conceal so proud a beauty? Who do you hide from in the deep blue sea?

VALERIE: Never mind. I have stopped being a fish.

Light changes back to previous

BIKEMAN: My compliments on your decision.

VALERIE: [*Progressively, she sounds more and more like the younger girl she really is.*] A fish could get lonely. And even lost.

BIKEMAN: It is a big sea out there.

VALERIE: And even if you had other fish with you, they'd only be other stupid little fish—except for bigger fish that might eat you—

BIKEMAN: Unless you were the biggest fish yourself—

VALERIE: But then you'd have to spend all your time eating littler fish—ugh!—and one day you would get caught or even harpooned.

BIKEMAN: Yes, it's been known to happen.

VALERIE: [*Brightening*] I would be a poison fish!

BIKEMAN: A poison fish! So, if anybody tried to eat *you*—

VALERIE: I'd murder their tummies! Die, harpooner, die! [*Quickly sobering up, and trying to sound again like DAISY.*] Bikeman, take me someplace else. Some place I have never been.

BIKEMAN: We won't need the bicycle. [*He offers his arm. She takes it. They stroll together and will wind up by the bed.*]

VALERIE: Where are we now? Where are we going?

BIKEMAN: Close your eyes so you can see. [*She does*]

VALERIE: I see tomorrow.

BIKEMAN: Tell me about it.

VALERIE: I know it's tomorrow because I am still me but I have a house of my own. And children. Four children. And a dog, a new dog. No, make that the same old dog, but in tomorrow he is new again.

BIKEMAN: Snuffy?

VALERIE: How did you know? I have a husband, too. If you are such a smarty-pants, tell me what my husband looks like.

BIKEMAN: Your husband—why, he would have to be quite a distinguished man. Very handsome. Very strong. Very smart. Very much like me.

VALERIE: All right, so he *is* something like you, but he is not so stuck up about it! Oh, look, at the fireplace! Have you ever seen such a rosy, cozy, crackling little fire!

They have reached the bed. VALERIE appears tired, even feeble. Gently, BIKEMAN helps her up on bed. She lies on her side, facing the "fireplace," her eyes closed.

BIKEMAN: Feeling comfortable?

VALERIE: Mmm-hmmm. Tomorrow is a very comfortable place to live in. Far away is all right, too.

BIKEMAN: And long ago?

VALERIE: Yes, I think that's my favorite. [*Sleepily*] Long ago. [*Drops her head on the pillow*] Long ago . . . and tomorrow. So rosy and cozy.

BIKEMAN: Daisy could live in the heart of the fire.

VALERIE: I could swim in the heart of the fire.

BIKEMAN: Daisy could swim in the heart of the flower of the fire.

VALERIE: So rosy and cozy.

BIKEMAN: [*Removing her bonnet, stroking her hair*] Tomorrow and long ago. Long ago and tomorrow . . . And all you need to do—Well, but you know all you need to do—

VALERIE: Close my eyes and see. Close my eyes and swim. Swim to the heart of the flower of the fire.

BIKEMAN: Yes . . . *yes!*

VALERIE, eyes closed, reaches her arms out toward the fire, makes a swimming motion—BIKEMAN, excited, nods encouragement. He has crouched low to be at her eye level. But suddenly, she opens her eyes and stares at him.

VALERIE: I know you, sir.

BIKEMAN: [*Quietly*] Yes, I know that you know me, ma'am.

VALERIE: [*Handing him her bonnet*] You may take my bonnet. You may take my parasol. I will not be requiring any further services of you.

BIKEMAN: At this time . . .

VALERIE: At this time. [*She raises herself up on an elbow and gazes at the "fireplace."*] Is it so rosy, then, Bikeman?

BIKEMAN places bonnet atop the parasol, brings it to his shoulder in a military gesture, salutes her with his free hand. Turns about smartly and marches off stage.

VALERIE: Is it so cozy? [*As scared little girl waking up from a bad dream*] Mom! Mommy! Dad!

Telephone voiceover of Doctor Stern:

I wish I could be more encouraging, Mrs. Leonard. The new meds have not been as effective as we had hoped. But let me assure you. Let me assure you.

Blue spot rises on VALERIE

VALERIE: [*Precariously controlled anxiety*] Tomorrow and tomorrow and tomorrow—is a pretty creepy place—and—Romeo—whereforth art thou not to be—(singing) "I'm half crazy"—and the other half of me is pretty crazy too. I pledge allegiance to *anything*. Give us this day our daily—No, just give us this day. And then maybe another day, if you don't awfully mind.

Offstage BIKEMAN whistles "Daisy" to diminuendo

DR. STERN: Let me assure you

VALERIE: [*Singing*] "Give you my answer true." [*Wearily*] Let me assure you.

Blackout

Labyrinth I: Little Pink Gloves

Characters: VALERIE, MOM, DAD, BROTHER, NURSE

Blackout

Blue follow spot for VALERIE rises as she kneels on the bed, hugging herself, staring, lost, looking scared.

Solo piano music (Chopin's "Raindrop" prelude)will begin when she moves, stop when she stops, accompanying her throughout the scene.

VALERIE rises from the bed, still hugging herself. As she does so, three faces become visible [illuminated by flashlights] at various widely separated places in the otherwise dark stage. The faces will not change location; VALERIE is the one who moves. BROTHER wears a baseball cap. Walking slowly, searchingly, through the dark, VALERIE will eventually extend her arms . . . reaching for, feeling for the others.

As VALERIE first approaches MOM, reaching out, MOM raises one hand in a withdrawing/repelling gesture, and averts her face. The raised hand is clad in a pink glove. The gloved hand can be seen as the face disappears.

VALERIE tries to approach DAD, again, walking as though through a difficult labyrinth. As she comes within arm's length of DAD, he raises both hands and crosses them above his head, as though warding off a vampire [flashlight is tucked into shirt]. And again, the hands are clad in pink gloves.

VALERIE inspects herself, as though asking: what's wrong with me? And, then, as though asking audience . . .

She is relieved to notice her brother. He is in profile, facing her. Chewing gum. She waves at him. Tries to reach him through the labyrinth. But as she nears him, BROTHER turns to the opposite profile and covers his face with a baseball glove. This glove is also clad in pink.

All the face-lights are suddenly extinguished.

VALERIE reaches out in one direction, then another. Then she crosses slowly back to the bed. She slumps next to the bed, her head and arms resting on the bed.

Lighting change to normal in bed area only. Blackout elsewhere.

NURSE approaches VALERIE with covered food tray. [We do not yet see her hands] Friendly smile. Sets tray on bedside table. With pink gloved hands, she starts to raise the lid.

Blackout

The Bible Lady Blues

Characters: ALL THREE THANATRICS, BIBLE LADY, VALERIE, GODLY VOICE, DAD's VOICE

AT RISE: Three hooded THANATRICS cross stage right to left in procession. They carry signs mounted on sticks: we cannot yet see the messages. Just before existing into opposite wings, THANATRIC I displays the sign: THE WORLD WILL END TOMORROW. Shakes a fist at audience, then exits.

THANATRIC II approaches exit, and displays sign: 185 SHOPPING DAYS UNTIL CHRISTMAS and waves cheerily. THANATRIC III approaches exit, and displays sign: THE BIBLE LADY BLUES

Examines with curiosity the sign he's been carrying, shrugs, and starts to exit, but almost collides with—

BIBLE LADY, who is attempting to bustle on stage, carrying a stool in front of her. She is a terribly sincere individual—in a highly professional manner—but somewhat overdressed in somewhat out of date fashion, just approaching the threshold of caricature. They do a momentary confused shuffle, each trying to maintain right of way. Finally, THANATRIC III exits and BIBLE LADY gains entry. They cast malignant looks at each other in passing.

BIBLE LADY beams at audience as she seeks a good place to set up her stool. Selects a forward position near same side of stage.

BIBLE LADY: Valerie! Come along now, dear! [*To audience*] My heart goes out to the little ones. Valerie!

VALERIE enters. BIBLE LADY pats the seat of the stool. VALERIE approaches the stool as she is beamed upon by BIBLE LADY. Just as VALERIE is ready to take the seat, BIBLE LADY installs herself on the stool and sighs.

BIBLE LADY: I know you have questions, my dear. The answers [*taps Bible*] are all here and in our hearts.

VALERIE: Yes, Miss Bible Lady.
BIBLE LADY: You do have questions?
VALERIE: Oh, yes, Miss Bible Lady, I do.
BIBLE LADY: What is your question, dear?
VALERIE: Why do kids have to die?
BIBLE LADY: Isn't it just fascinating, the kind of questions that children will ask! So, what is your question, dear?
VALERIE: Kids—why do kids have to die?
BIBLE LADY: Go ahead, dear, don't be shy. Ask your question.
VALERIE: [Patiently overarticulating] Why do kids have to die? Why do I have to die?
BIBLE LADY: [Beaming] Whatever your question, my dear, the answer is in our hearts and, here, in this book.
VALERIE: May I see the book, please?
BIBLE LADY: Oh, but of course! Open this book to any page and the answers will come tumbling out. [Confidingly] I myself was once troubled and confused. I found my new life in the Bible.
VALERIE: [Opens Bible, apparently at random. Reads aloud as she scans through it]
                "The Book of Judges" Judges! OK, judges must know a lot of stuff. Let's see: "and they pursued after him, and caught him, and cut off his thumbs and his great toes." What are "great toes," Bible Lady? Are those like big toes?
BIBLE LADY: Yes, one and the same. Or, should I say, two and the same!
VALERIE: OK, and next thing it says is that somebody said, Adonibezek said, um, "Three score and ten kings, having their thumbs and great toes cut off, gathered their food under his table." I guess that means under Adonibezek's table, and that was probably hard to do with their thumbs and great toes cut off. I wonder what they did with all those cut-off thumbs and great toes?
BIBLE LADY: I've wondered about that myself.
VALERIE: [Flipping pages, scanning] Wow, this is good stuff! Listen—

THANATRICS peek out and start to converge slowly on VALERIE and BIBLE LADY to hear better.

VALERIE: "But when the children of Israel cried unto Jehovah, Jehovah raised them up a saviour." Boy, that's what we need around here, a saviour!

BIBLE LADY: Jesus! Sweet Jesus!

VALERIE: Well, here it says the saviour was "Ehud the son of Gera, the Benjamite, a man left-handed." A left-handed saviour. Wow! I'm left-handed! Maybe I could be a saviour, too!

BIBLE LADY: Ladies can be saints if they're very amazingly good and also Roman Catholics.

VALERIE: Only men get to be saviours? That's not fair.

BIBLE LADY: Ah, but that's the way it is, dear. Anyhow, I don't think you need to continue with that Ehud person.

VALERIE: Oh, but listen Miss Bible Lady! This looks like it's going to get really intense. "And Ehud made him a sword which had two edges, and he girded it under his robe upon his right thigh. And he offered the tribute unto Eglon, king of Moab; now Eglon was a very fat man." [*Laughs*] "Now Eglon was a very fat man." It says so right here in the Bible!

BIBLE LADY: He may have had a glandular problem.

THANATRICS now are gathered behind VALERIE, trying to read over her shoulder.

VALERIE: "And Ehud came unto him; and he was sitting by himself alone in the cool upper room." I bet he's going to get his thumbs chopped off, and his great toes, too, and who knows what else.

BIBLE LADY: [*Snatches book away from VALERIE and continues the reading aloud*]: "And Ehud said, I have a message from God unto thee." You see, dear, it's perfectly all right. He had a message from God.

VALERIE: [*Snatching the book back herself. As she describes the action, the THANATRICS try to follow and emulate it.*] "And Ehud put forth his left hand, and took the sword from his right thigh, and thrust it into his body" Argh! Ehud thrust the sword into his own body? Why would a left-handed saviour do that?

THAN I:	I don't think that's what they meant. I think they meant he thrust the sword into Eglon's body.
VALERIE:	Then why didn't they say so? My teacher would mark me down if I wrote like that. Well, maybe you're right though: "and thrust it into his body . . . and the fat closed upon the blade."
THAN II:	Does it really say that?
VALERIE:	[*Emphasizing the grisly deed with special relish*] "And the fat closed upon the blade, for he drew not the sword out of his body; and it came out behind."

THANs disport themselves in horror and delight.

	That was a message from God?
BIBLE LADY:	Oh, the Bible is full of surprises, dear. You see how a message from God can take many different forms.
VALERIE:	Oh, I see, I see!
THAN I:	I don't see!
THAN II & III:	I don't see!
VALERIE:	Very fat Eglon must have thought, "Oh, good, here's a nice message from God." But the message was Ehud's sword with two edges. So it's like leukemia. Leukemia is God's message to kids.
BIBLE LADY:	No, my dear, I wouldn't put it that way. Eglund was a nasty old king who believed in the wrong God.
VALERIE:	It doesn't say he was old. I guess he was nasty, though.
BIBLE LADY:	God has to be tough with the wrong kind of people. But God's message is love, not leukemia. God's message is everlasting love, not death.

THANs to each other:

THAN III:	Hey, this is getting deep—
THAN II:	Too deep for me—
THAN I:	Keep it down, will you? I want to hear how this comes out.
VALERIE:	So it's love when God gives kids leukemia?
BIBLE LADY:	God doesn't actually *give* kids leukemia.
VALERIE:	Well, He doesn't exactly *not* give kids leukemia, either.

BIBLE LADY: It may not be easy for children to understand such things.

Sound: Crack of thunder. Howling winds. All react. Lights waver, temporary darkness, followed by restoration of light

VOICE:	[*As diminished wind sounds continue*] Perhaps I can help.
THAN I:	It's The Big Guy.
THAN II:	You're Number One, Big Guy.
THAN III:	You've always been Number One with me!
BIBLE LADY:	Oh, my!
VALERIE:	Yes, perhaps you can help. We could use a few explanations around here.
VOICE:	I don't *have* to explain anything.
VALERIE:	But you will, won't you? For a kid? I don't need to know *everything*. Just a little.
THAN II:	Valerie—ask Him—ah!—ask Him if dogs and cats go to the same heaven!
THAN III:	What a stupid question! Ask Him, "Does the rain have a father?"
THAN I:	Creation! Ask him about creation! I've got a bet down!
VOICE:	One question, and from Valerie. There—I've turned the wind machine down so you can think clearly. [*Wind sounds end*]
VALERIE:	Oh, that's a relief. One question!

All go into a football-type huddle. Some mutterings and disagreements. Finally, VALERIE claps her hand and they break cleanly from the huddle. VALERIE steps forward as the others fan out behind her.

VOICE:	You have chosen the question? You are sure this is the one question you want me to answer? Very well.
VALERIE:	Is this happening to me because I'm a bad little girl, or because you are a bad old God?

A tableau immediately forms. All characters listen in frozen hyper-suspense.

VOICE:	Go ahead, Valerie. Just ask me the question. [*Windsounds start again, will gradually become louder*]

VALERIE:	I just asked you the question.
VOICE:	Yes, the question. Speak up! And be quick about it!
VALERIE:	[*Shouting over the wind*] Is this happening to me because I'm a bad little girl—

Blackout

VOICE:	Speak up, child!
VALERIE:	—or because you're a bad old God?

Windsounds build to crescendo, then silence.

Blue follow spot rises on VALERIE. She is now the only person on stage. Still holding the Bible, she walks slowly toward her bed. Places Bible on the bedside table. On second thought, places Bible inside the drawer. Sits at table and pensively starts to comb her hair. After a moment, while combing:

VALERIE: I should have expected that. Why should The Big Guy, why should Number One tell me any of his secrets? [*Smiles sadly.*] That's OK. I have some secrets of my own. I guess everybody does. But my best secrets are really something intense. Maybe The Big Guy needs his secrets as much as I need mine. Anyhow, what's so great about knowing? [*Stops combing her hair.*] Even if I keep asking, "why, why, why, why!" and even if they kept answering, "because this, because that," and even if "because this" and "because that" was really the truth, I'd still be here like this, wouldn't I? And I would be thinking, "So, that's why this, and that's why that!" But I still wouldn't be home. And I still wouldn't be back in school. And I still wouldn't be seeing my friends. And I'd still be scared. [*Resumes and completes combing.*]

Still, I do want to know! [*Climbs into bed. Slips under the covers.*] Judges. That's in the Old Testament. And that's where they tell about Jephthah and his daughter. I've never known a real Jephthah, but this Jephthah seems pretty real to me sometimes. And especially his daughter. She is more real than ever lately. [*Reaches into bedside table, opens drawer, retrieves Bible.*]

OK. If nobody will give me the answers, then I'll be Miss Wise Guy of Planet Earth. First, you have to know about Jephthah. And about Jephthah's daughter. [*She holds up the Bible and raps it sharply.*]

VOICE OF
BIBLE LADY: Ahem!

VALERIE raps Bible again

BIBLE LADY: "Now Jephthah, the Gileadutem was a mighty man of valor—"

VALERIE: Hear that? A mighty man of valor. But probably not left-handed.

BIBLE LADY: "And it came to pass . . . that when the children of Ammon made war against Israel, the elders of Gilead went to fetch Jephthah . . . and they said, 'Come and be our chief, that we might fight with the children of Ammon'."

VALERIE: I know what you're thinking. Why were children fighting, and who would care? But those would be big children, like my mother is a grown up and she's still *her* mother's child. Kinda confusing, but it's the Bible and you have to make some allowances for how they say things. Now, Miss Bible Lady, get to the Spirit of Jehovah part, please.

BIBLE LADY: "Then the Spirit of Jehovah came upon Jephthah . . . And Jephthah vowed a vow unto Jehovah, and said, 'If thou wilt indeed deliver the children of Ammon into my hand, then it shall be, that whatsoever cometh forth from the doors of my house to meet me when I return . . . it shall be Jehovah's, and I will offer it up for a burnt offering' "

VALERIE: I hope you've been paying attention: "whatsoever cometh forth from the doors of my house to meet me when I

	return . . . it shall be Jehovah's, and I will offer it up for a burnt offering."
BIBLE LADY:	"So Jephthah passed over unto the children of Ammon to fight against them; and Jehovah delivered them into his hand. And he smote them . . . even twenty cities . . . with a very great slaughter. So the children of Ammon were subdued before the children of Israel."
VALERIE:	And what happens then? What happens then? Would you believe it!
BIBLE LADY:	"And Jephthah came . . . unto his house, and behold, his daughter came out to meet him with timbrels and with dances: and she was his only child."
VALERIE:	"Hi, Dad! Sure good to see you! Wash the blood off your hands and we'll have supper!"
BIBLE LADY:	"And he said, 'Alas, my daughter! Thou hast brought me very low'."
VALERIE:	I hast? All I did was come out and say, "Hi, Dad!" and do a happy little dance.
FATHER'S VOICE:	I told The Big Guy I would give him whatsoever came out of my house first.
VALERIE:	And I'm "whatsoever!" And you're giving me to Jehovah!
FATHER'S VOICE:	As a burnt offering.
VALERIE:	Oh!
FATHER'S VOICE:	I'm really sorry about this, kid.
VALERIE:	Me, too, Dad. Well, you did give your word . . .
FATHER'S VOICE:	I'm glad you understand. So . . . what's for supper?

THANs return bearing token pieces of wood and a torch.

VALERIE:	Jephthah's daughter went into the mountains with some companions. What did she do there? She bewailed her virginity. No kidding! I guess that's what virgins did in those days. Bewailed.

THANs continue with their preparations.

VALERIE: [*To THANs*] You're really going to burn me, aren't you?
THAN I: It looks that way.
THAN II: That's our instructions.
VALERIE: Alive? Are you going to burn me *alive?*
THAN I: I don't know. What does the Bible say?

VALERIE raps Bible again and again.

VOICE OF
BIBLE LADY: On this point, the Bible is silent.
VALERIE: Any chance of a last minute rescue?

THANs look sadly at each other.

VALERIE: Jehovah says, "Aw, Jephthah, you really don't have to
              burn your daughter just to please me. The thought is
              enough. Or Jephthah says, "Can't we talk this over? How
              about I write a new song for you, or build a temple?
              Or slaughter another batch of Ammonites?"
THAN I: I'm afraid not.
VALERIE: Maybe it will rain.
THAN III: I've read Judges over and over again, and, there's noth-
              ing about rain either.
VALERIE: Oh. Well, does it say that I die bravely?
THAN III: There's nothing about that, one way or another.
VALERIE: Does it say that I don't feel any pain?
THAN II: Nothing about that either.
VALERIE: Oh, golly! Well, does it say that people cried and were
              very sad, especially my Dad. And that maybe God was
              kinda sad, too, and wished he hadn't done it?

THANs all shake heads and gesture in the negative.

VALERIE: [*Gathering up all her resources*] OK, then! Maybe you
              burn me alive. And maybe it hurts real bad. And maybe
              I'm not too brave about it. And maybe nobody cries
              and says they will miss me. And maybe Dad goes off
              to play golf. And—and maybe God doesn't think he's
              done anything wrong to let this happen. *But!* But you

see—something good really comes out of it after all—right?

THANs react in confusion.

I mean, when people think about this! How a Daddy kept his word to God even though he had to kill his own daughter. And how a daughter said, "OK, Daddy and God know best!" This will just have to make things better. It will just have to make people better. I mean, everybody will realize that it's stupid to kill each other and be mean to each other, so what's one girl's death if it makes the whole world a better place for ever and ever! There! Now that makes sense, doesn't it? [*Triumphantly*] That's what it all means!

THAN I: It sounds might fine to me, young lady.

THAN III to [*sotto voce*] But in Judges 12 the slaughter starts all over
THAN II: again. Her ashes are probably still floating in the air . . .

VALERIE: And good people will remember my name for always and forever. Oh—what *is* my name?

THAN I lights the torch.

VOICE OF Child, you are the daughter of Jephthah. The Bible gives
BIBLE LADY: you *no* name.

VALERIE: [*Voice rising in desperation.*] What is my name? What is my name?

Blackout

Scene-changing music

Labyrinth II: Whatsoever

SETTING AT RISE: Apart from the ever-present bed, the only other object on stage is a closed door in its frame: right smack in stage center.

Music ends

Two THANATRICS enter from opposite wings. They are walking backwards stealthfully and sprinkling imaginary breadcrumbs along the paths they have been taking.

As THANATRICS pass each other:

THAN I: [*Derisively*] Breadcrumbs, I suppose! You think bread-crumbs will help you find your way back!

THAN II: Yes, breadcrumbs! I see you're doing the same!

THAN I: Not the same at all, not the same at all!

THAN II: Yes, the same! Just the same!

THAN I: Your crumbs will be eaten by birds and then they will be eaten by squirrels. Where will you be then? How will you find your way back?

THAN II: If my crumbs are eaten by birds and if my crumbs are eaten by squirrels, then so will yours. And where will *you* be then? And how will you find *your* way back?

THAN I: See for yourself—

BIRD-THAN appears, adorned with a few token feathers and a beak. Hops about, excited about both crumb trails. Trying to decide which to sample first. Pecks at one of THAN II's crumbs. Makes evaluative response—not bad, but not great either. Then pecks at one of THAN II's crumbs. Mmmm! Connoisseur's response of approval. Takes another peck. Suddenly looks unwell, clutches at its stomach, staggers about a moment, then faces audience for soliloquy, delivered with stagey eloquence.

BIRD-THAN: No! This cannot be!

THAN I: [*Furtive whisper*] Why, that's Stage 1!

BIRD-THAN: [*Glaring at THAN II*] Prithee away, morbid vision—ooh! I am so pecked off at you!

THAN II:	Stage 2 and counting. . . .
BIRD-THAN:	[*Flapping wings in futile desperation*]
	"Alas, 'tis true I have gone here and there
	And made myself a motley to the view,
	Gored my own thoughts, sold cheap what is most dear,
	Made old offenses of affections new . . ."
THAN I:	Ah! A new stage: overacting!
BIRD-THAN:	"Most true it is that I have look'd on truth
	Askance and strangely: but, by all above—
	give my heart another youth . . ."
THAN I:	Oh, it's just plain old Stage 3 after all, Shakespearized.
THAN II:	And here comes Depression—
BIRD-THAN:	[*Settling down gracefully to perish*] "Beauty, truth, and rarity, Grace in all simplicity, Here lie . . ."
THAN I:	Wrong sequence! Acceptance *after* Depression.
BIRD-THAN:	Not for birds of my feather. "And death is now the phoenix's nest." Lesser Shakespeare, perhaps, but Shakespeare nevertheless. [*Completes luxurious dying with a final ruffle of feathers*]
THAN I:	You see, then, the superiority of my method
THAN II:	Poisoning our little feathery and furry friends is superior?
THAN I:	Your trail will be invisible by morning. My trail will be beautifully delineated by dead birds and dead squirrels and dead come-what-mays

THANs I and II exchange jibes as they continue crumb-tossing their ways to opposite wing exits.

THAN II:	A stupid method!
THAN I:	A beautiful method!

Door opens from the inside. VALERIE stands just inside the threshold.

VALERIE:	Dad? [*Looks about anxiously, notices defunct BIRD-THAN*] No Dad. No Mom. And it must have been raining dead birds again. I thought that was only a dream.
MOM:	[*Standing up in audience*] I thought that was only a dream. People wake up from dreams.

DAD: [*Standing up in a different part of the audience*] People wake up from bad dreams.

VALERIE: Mom? Dad? I'm here. I'm right here.

MOM and DAD approach stage.

MOM: I just can't reach her lately. No matter how I try. She seems so distant.

VALERIE: Right here, Mom.

DAD: It *is* a bad dream. We will all wake up from it one of these days, and she will be just fine. We will all be just fine. This sort of thing doesn't happen to people like us.

VALERIE: Right here, Dad.

MOM and DAD now on stage. Labyrinth music begins

MOM and DAD each seek VALERIE, moving separately in conjunction with music and as though through an invisible labyrinth. Occasionally one or the other encounters a barrier and must retrace steps and start again. Occasionally one parent comes very close to VALERIE, but fails to see her.

MOM: Valerie? Where is that girl?

DAD passes by MOM without seeming to recognize or acknowledge her.

DAD: Valerie, where's my Little Pumpkin? Valerie?

MOM: I am losing . . . well . . . everybody

DAD: That's enough now! Come out! Come out wherever you are!

VALERIE: I can't come *out.* Don't you see, Dad? Mom? I can't come *out.*

DAD: Where is that child?

MOM: Where is everybody?

DAD: I'm losing patience with you! Come here!

Labyrinth music ends

VALERIE: "Whatsoever cometh forth from the doors will be offered up for a burnt offering." You see, I can't come out. Don't make me.

MOM and DAD, resigned and fretting in their own ways, slowly cross in opposite directions away from VALERIE. They will remain at opposite sides of stage, lost in their own thoughts. Meanwhile, noticed only by VALERIE, the BIRD-THAN stirs a little, ruffles its feathers, and gradually returns to life.

VALERIE: [*To BIRD-THAN*] That's a good trick, you know. A really good trick.

BIRD-THAN: Easy for a phoenix.

VALERIE: I wish I could do that. I wish I was a phoenix and not a whatsoever.

BIRD-THAN: [*Now feeling perky and sporting about*] Not everybody can be a phoenix. But what's so bad about being a whatsoever?

VALERIE: If you're a whatsoever, you can't come out.

BIRD-THAN: The door is open

VALERIE: But you still can't come out because how can you come out when even if you come out it wouldn't be *you* who comes out?

BIRD-THAN: I don't understand.

VALERIE: I don't understand it that well myself, bird-brain! I just know that Valerie has burrowed so deep down inside me, like a small animal, that she can't just come out even when she wants to.

BIRD-THAN: Burrowed down so deep inside, like a small animal!

VALERIE: And the Me that's left over can only hurt and be done things to.

BIRD-THAN: Ah!

VALERIE: Most of the left-over is the Doctor's Me and the Nurse's Me. It's the Other-People-Doing-All-Kinds-of-Scary-Things-to-Me Me.

BIRD-THAN: But what about Mom and Dad?

VALERIE: Sure. [*Pause*] There's Mom's Me, too, and there's Dad's Me. I worked hard to be those Me's for them. Now it's *real* hard. They want their Me's to come out.

BIRD-THAN: But they're not Valerie.

VALERIE: She's hiding even from me.

BIRD-THAN: You may be right—I think it's easier being a phoenix!

VALERIE: After you die and do your trick, are you the same phoenix?

BIRD-THAN: Why, what a question! I suppose so. But that's only supposing. I really have no idea. I don't remember a thing about it.

VALERIE: I remember just being Valerie. And dancing through doors.

BIRD-THAN: Dance now! Come through the door and dance with me!

VALERIE: I can't.

BIRD-THAN: Oh, you can so, too! Come, dance with me!

New music begins: BIRD-THAN starts to dance invitingly.

VALERIE: But you see, I simply can't! I am only this left-over Me that has no place to hide. I . . . I don't even have a name any more!

BIRD-THAN: Dance . . . dance!

BIRD-THAN's dancing becomes more demanding and aggressive

VALERIE: [*Dancing within the doorway, almost but not quite stepping through*] Don't make me dance! Please!

BIRD-THAN and VALERIE execute a brief slow motion mime-dance in which BIRD-THAN makes several efforts to catch hold of her, and she just manages to avoid him. Finally, BIRD-THAN displays a flamboyant maneuver and comes to a halt with a frozen grotesque stance, facing VALERIE.

VALERIE: Ooooh!

BIRD-THAN now whirls around and confronts the audience: he has no face.

Music ends

VALERIE: My goodness! You certainly do get around! How is Grandmother?

BIRD-THAN: That old girl? You might be surprised!
VALERIE: I bet *she* has a name of her very own. Well, that settles it!
BIRD-THAN: What settles what, Little Pumpkin?
VALERIE: I won't dance with anyone—least of all with you—until I have a name of my own. Wait—until I have my *own* name back! Until I am My Me!

VALERIE closes her door and disappears from view. BIRD-THAN departs swiftly.

MOM and DAD have been thinking all this time. They are in a more centered and matured mood as they move to within an arm's length of each other, near the door.

DAD: Did I hear a door slam?
MOM: Look there's a door in that wall.

MOM and DAD take each other's hands and face the door.

DAD: I wonder who lives here.
MOM: It may be somebody we know.
       [*They approach the door.*]
VOICE OF
THAN I: How will you find your way back?
VOICE OF
THAN II: How will you find *your* way back?

Blackout

Proceed at Your Own Risk

Characters: THANATRIC I, THANATRIC II, VALERIE, BIBLE LADY,
REALITY MAN

AT RISE: THAN I enters, wearing bright yellow construction hard hat and carrying a saw horse type of road barrier. Sets it up. THAN II, similarly hatted, follows promptly and posts a sign: THIS SCENE UNDER CON-STRUCTION while THAN I exits and returns with a second barrier. THAN II then uses THAN I's back as drawing board while completing another sign. This sign is then attached to second barrier: PROCEED AT YOUR OWN RISK. THANs pause to admire their work and saunter off in satisfied, good fellowship mode.

VALERIE, clad in sloppy jeans outfit, strolls on, soft drink and script in hand. She seats herself on a saw horse, flips through the script until she finds the place she wants, and reads. BIBLE LADY soon joins her, also casually dressed and with her copy of script, seats herself on the other barrier.

BIBLE LADY:	So: where are we?
VALERIE:	You tell me. I'd say our first problem is in the saviour dialogue.
BIBLE LADY:	My line, probably. "Ladies can be saints if they're very amazingly good and also Roman Catholics."
VALERIE:	This may be out of character for you. Sounds more like something I would say.
BIBLE LADY:	And the line just calls too much attention to itself.
VALERIE:	But maybe your character is trying to unbend a little and talk at my level or pick upon my style. You know, "very amazingly good."
BIBLE LADY:	I see what you mean.
VALERIE:	But that line is a mouthful.
BIBLE LADY:	We might lose focus instead of moving straight ahead.
VALERIE:	Exactly. And I don't see where that Roman Catholic business is so important. I mean, what are we getting at here?
BIBLE LADY:	I feel everything is moving toward the uncovering of your identity crisis, if you don't mind the jargon.

VALERIE:	Uh-huh. Really not just my identity crisis, though. Everybody's, maybe.
BIBLE LADY:	Religion's not helping. I try to persuade you that all the answers are here in the Bible, but instead you discover that a girl—
VALERIE:	A good girl—
BIBLE LADY:	Yes, a good little girl, a daughter can die for no good reason.
VALERIE:	It's OK with Dad. It's OK with God. At least, it's OK enough for them to let this happen. So what's a kid to think?
BIBLE LADY:	[*Slipping into her character's voice and tone*] "You die tomorrow without a name, dear. Sweet dreams!"
VALERIE:	OK. So let's move on this.

REALITY MAN enters and observes the scene for a while. He holds an attache case and is dressed as a mainstream corporate type: quality suit, tie, ostentatiously shiny shoes. VALERIE and BIBLE LADY do not acknowledge his presence.

BIBLE LADY:	Line!
VALERIE:	"A left-handed saviour. Wow! I'm left-handed! Maybe I could be a saviour, too!"
BIBLE LADY:	"Ladies can be saints."
VALERIE:	Better! Much better. But the real problem here, I think is not so much with this scene itself, but with what it does or doesn't do for where we're going with the whole thing.
BIBLE LADY:	I feel OK about the tone and the transitions. There's momentum, too, but it's not of the straight-ahead kind.
VALERIE:	This scene just keeps swerving, the whole play, too. Yet it snaps around the turns and seems to pick up nasty little energies as it keeps twisting around the bend.
BIBLE LADY:	Too much for the audience?
VALERIE:	They can handle it, I think. It's not the dinner theater crowd. But I still wonder if this scene takes us far enough. I suspect the author is just trying to do too much in an hour.

BIBLE LADY: I agree. So I've been thinking, what if we—no! That's a pretty dumb idea now that I think of it again.

VALERIE: What's a pretty dumb idea?

BIBLE LADY: Oh, let's forget it.

VALERIE: Come on—out with it.

BIBLE LADY: Well, suppose first what if we give ourselves a little more time by scrapping you-know-what-scene—

VALERIE: Go on—

BIBLE LADY: And what we would do instead is return to BIBLE LADY BLUES.

VALERIE: You mean, do it as written, and then come back to the same scene? Go on—

REALITY MAN: Ladies, may I introduce myself—

They glance at him, but return immediately to their work.

BIBLE LADY: We pick up the scene in progress, say, where we did just now. And after just a moment, to establish it, we break off.

VALERIE: We don't like the way it's going! "Let's do it over and this time get the scene right!"

BIBLE LADY: Maybe we argue. Fly into rage. A good, healthy cat fight.

REALITY MAN: My card, ladies—

VALERIE: "Argue with you—don't make me laugh! You, you soap opera reject, you!"

BIBLE LADY: "Buzz off, doll-baby!"

VALERIE: "You don't have the technique for a quality script."

BIBLE LADY: "Technique! I can technique rings around you any day, and any night, too, I might add!"

VALERIE: "Buzzard!"

BIBLE LADY: "Barbie doll!" Well, that was refreshing. But—back to the script.

REALITY MAN: [*Still polite, but more insistent*] I do not wish to disturb you, ladies, but permit me to introduce myself and explain my business—

VALERIE and BIBLE LADY give him "Would you please just go away" looks.

VALERIE:	OK. What's your concept.
BIBLE LADY:	What we have here in reality—
REALITY MAN:	Ah!
BIBLE LADY:	is a girl with leukemia. She's confined to an isolation unit. Alone. Almost untouchable.
VALERIE:	Uh-huh.
BIBLE LADY:	She might die.
VALERIE:	She knows that.
BIBLE LADY:	Meanwhile, she has a lot to put up with and a lot to try to make sense of. And so does the audience.
VALERIE:	Nobody's answers are working very well. I follow. So?
REALITY MAN:	[*Approaching VALERIE and flashing a wallet-badge at her. Reluctantly, she looks at it.*] I don't think this has to be too unpleasant for any of us.
BIBLE LADY:	[*In actorish low-life voice*] Jeez! Are we busted? Get me my mouthpiece. Flatfoot—I don't say a word without my mouthpiece. Don't give your right name, Mildred!
REALITY MAN:	I am not a police officer. I am not here to "bust" you. And I have been told my feet are exquisite.
BIBLE LADY:	Well, your timing's not. We have a show to do.
REALITY MAN:	Of that I am well aware. It is my reason for being here.
VALERIE:	The badge says something about a realty bureau. We're not buying or selling houses.
REALITY MAN:	Not realty. *Reality.* Bureau of Reality Enforcement.
BIBLE LADY:	Realty, reality. What's the difference? I lived in reality once. A nice place to visit—no, not even a nice place to visit: it's all yours, Flatfoot!
REALITY MAN:	Since you are busy and I am busy, why don't we just do what needs to be done and try to be civilized about it?
VALERIE:	Or else—or else, what?
REALITY MAN:	Oh, we needn't speak of or else's. I do have the power vested in me by the appropriate authorities, but it needn't come to that.
BIBLE LADY:	OK—just spit it out, Flatfoot!
REALITY MAN:	[*Opens attache case and withdraws a document*] Is this document known to you?
VALERIE:	It's a script. It's our script. How did you get a copy?

REALITY MAN: Ah, we do have our ways. You admit this is your script, then?

VALERIE: We didn't write it.

BIBLE LADY: [*Mock agitation*] "Oh, officer, they're making us do it! Kidnapped me mother! Never see the dear old dotty thing again if we don't do this daft little script!"

REALITY MAN: Oh, say, you are *acting,* aren't you? How charming! But you are not in difficulty, not either one of you. I am here with the one firm purpose in mind

BIBLE LADY: [*Mock seductress, accompanied by sensuous body-protective gestures*] "Oh, I know your one firm purpose in mind. But you shan't have me! Shan't, shan't, shan't!"

VALERIE: Is that your technique? Or your arthritis?

REALITY MAN: Perhaps I should simply read the complaint.

BIBLE LADY: Well, perhaps you simply should!

REALITY MAN: [*Produces a document from his jacket pocket. As he prepares to read it aloud, BIBLE LADY tugs on his sleeve and turns him toward the audience*] Bureau of Reality Enforcement. Complaint #DS 355-4382655. Oh! There's an audience here already! My! An audience!

[*Twinkles shyly at audience; BIBLE LADY is quietly detaching one of the title signs and reattaching it to his back as he goes on speaking*]

The good citizens of London, Ontario, Canada, acting in the interests of good citizens everywhere, hereby file this complaint against Pretty Desperate Productions re its scheduled performance of the play entitled, *"The Girl in the Raindrop."*

Now, mind you—this is an aside—I have nothing personal against theatrical enterprises. I believe that an edifying play can be, well, quite edifying. And there is no doubt in my mind but that involvement in theatrical enterprises does keep a certain number of unstable and unreliable characters from wandering about the streets

	or sounding their horns past 9 p.m. in good neighbor-hoods such as my own.
VALERIE:	The complaint?
REALITY MAN:	Ah, the complaint, yes! "The aforementioned play deviates from reality in several respects, as detailed on the following pages."

[He riffles through a sheaf of attached pages.]

Humm . . . hummm . . . hummm. Yes, in many, many respects. And so, if I may proceed to the conclusion: "This play should either be brought into compliance with existing reality laws and regulations or it should be torn apart furiously into a thousand thousand little pieces and burned to a crisp, and the ashes then force-fed to the drooling monster responsible for its author-ship."

VALERIE:	Am I mistaken, or does the objectivity fade just a bit at the very end?
REALITY MAN:	Well, it *is* a lengthy document and we have been run-ning a tad short in the objectivity department—the budget bureau trimmed our request again.
BIBLE LADY:	OK—just what exactly do you want us to do, Flatfoot?
REALITY MAN:	Ah, I have taken the liberty to prepare a few sug-gestions. The title is an appropriate place to begin. A girl will not fit into a raindrop. This is unrealistic, totally.
VALERIE:	A really small girl would fit—
BIBLE LADY:	—Into a really big raindrop
REALITY MAN:	Perhaps so. I will suspend that objection, for the moment.

VALERIE and BIBLE LADY come up on either side of REALITY MAN and each capture one of his arms.

VALERIE:	You are a man of the world. You know that reality belongs—well—in reality! Go back to the real world. I'm sure they need you there.
REALITY MAN:	Not so fast! There are many other complaints!
BIBLE LADY:	Reality is calling you! Listen—Can't you hear its big dull voice?

REALITY MAN: [*Listens*] That wasn't a bullfrog, then? For years I have been hearing a sort of phantom bullfrog croaking at me. But, it's Reality, you say! Wait—*I* do Reality here!

VALERIE: Can't we make a deal?

REALITY MAN: I am an honest man.

VALERIE: An honest deal! Show us what you find most unrealistic about this scene. If we can't change the scene or your mind, then we'll just cancel the performance.

REALITY MAN: You'll cancel the whole play? Ah? Yes, that sounds like a deal. But you will have to meet several objections, all closely related.

VALERIE: Agreed.

BIBLE LADY: Count me out! I've had about as much Reality as I can stand for one day! [*Stalks out, exits.*]

REALITY MAN: You theater people—such temperament!

VALERIE: Last I heard, temperament was still part of Reality. On with it!

REALITY MAN: And let the audience render judgment. *Vox populi über alles!* Audience people—examine this character as she now stands before you and as she has stood before you through every scene, rife with violations of Reality.

VALERIE: What's wrong with how I stand before you?

REALITY MAN: You are a refutation of the character you were engaged to portray! Oh, yes! Your character is a sickly young person who is confined to an isolation unit. But you flirt—you take a preposterous trip on a preposterous bicycle—you—you dance with a more than preposterous bird—and you dare to question the Almighty! Where is your illness? Where is all the Reality of it? [*Gloating*] I can sense the jury's verdict!

VALERIE: Oh, I'm guilty all right.

REALTY MAN: Ah!

VALERIE: Would you see me as I am? [*Crosses to the bed, pauses*] We wouldn't need the rest of the stage. Most of the other characters would not appear. No music, no lighting changes, no props. More medical equipment and paraphernalia, though. And there'd be that hospital smell, if it's Reality you want.

REALITY MAN approaches the bed.

REALITY MAN: All improvements! And now please improve the dialogue. I will show you how.

VALERIE slips into bed.

VALERIE: Sorry. This is a sterile unit. You can't enter. And neither can the audience.

REALITY MAN: Oh!

VALERIE: And often I don't have the energy to speak. The treatments take a lot out of me. Or the drugs will have made me drowsy.

REALITY MAN: So, what would you do, then?

VALERIE: Mostly what I'm doing now. Except we wouldn't be having this conversation, and I would be sort of painful to look at. Since I would be alone now, I probably would remove my wig.

REALITY MAN is standing as though at a boundary line, straining to stay in contact with her.

REALITY MAN: Wig? You're a girl! Barely a teenager!

VALERIE: Chemotherapy will do that. My hair has been falling out. How much of my Reality do you want in this play? There's more—and the more Reality the better, right?

REALITY MAN: Right! Ah, generally speaking! So there would be you and you would be in bed. Nothing very much would be happening.

VALERIE: Only living and dying.

REALITY MAN: And that might go on endlessly!

VALERIE: Not endlessly.

REALITY MAN: Ah! But you are thinking! Yes, you think!

VALERIE: Thank you.

REALITY MAN: Suppose we took your thoughts—yes, suppose we took your thoughts and—and *dramatized* them! You see, you see: something would happen then! We would have action, interaction, a play!

VALERIE: Now why didn't we think of that?

REALITY MAN, in his growing excitement, rushes across the "boundary" and up to the bed.

REALITY MAN: And—don't you see—there's no limit!? Your mind can be any place, every place!
VALERIE: Go away!
REALITY MAN: And—say, how's this—we can even dramatize the way that thought goes over and over the same situation. We can do the same scene over and over with interesting differences. And that will give it all so much more Reality!

VALERIE pulls an unseen cord attached to her bed. A "beep" sounds

THANs I and II, still wearing their hard hats, rush on stage. Take REALITY MAN by his arms and start to give him the bum's rush. As he is exiting,

 No, no! You're not Reality! Only her thoughts are real, don't you see? Careful! Don't step on my feet!
VALERIE: Your feet are exquisite.
REALITY MAN: [*From offstage*] Did you hear that? Exquisite!

Blue spot looks for VALERIE. It's a little confused and uncertain. She has to guide it over. Finally the blue spot has become her familiar companion again.

VALERIE: [*Sighs. To the blue spot*] Just you and me again, baby! Maybe we can even have us a little music again . . .

Music

Blackout

Places to Go

*Characters: DR. STERN (VOICE), MOM, THAN/CONSTRUCTION
WORKER (wearing hard hat), BIBLE LADY (carrying Bible), DAD
(carrying stuffed animal), REALITY MAN (carrying attache case),
VALERIE*

AT RISE: *Normal lighting. Occupant of the bed is burrowed down, lying
with face away from audience.*

VOICE: (DR. STERN) As a point of reference, the reverse precautions have been effective. You would not catch leukemia from Valerie. But we must be concerned with what Valerie might catch from you while her immune system is so compromised. Thank you for your understanding.

*Characters, other than VALERIE, start to filter onto stage from various
points of origin. They are purposeful, but relaxed, in no rush. The
unspoken attitude is "we are not actors anymore, just people." Within
a few moments, as DR. STERN continues, they will acknowledge each
other—quietly greet, shake hands, etc. and form a loose cluster. When they
speak to each other, it is also low key.*

           I sound just like a doctor, don't I? Believe me, it has taken years of practice. And now—it is not easy to stop sounding like a doctor! [*Sounding less professional as he goes along*] And, you know, I don't think they would want me to stop being the doctor. Not really. Somebody has to play this part, you know what I mean?

BIBLE LADY: [*To THAN*] I hope this scene is not under construction, too.

THAN: Yes, ma'am. No, ma'am.

BIBLE LADY: No, ma'am? Yes, ma'am?

REALITY MAN: [*THAN to BIBLE LADY*] I think he means that it's all worked out, but we won't see or hear the end of it.

BIBLE LADY: Has Reality Man become Riddle Man?

MOM: [*To DAD*] Who's your new friend?

DAD: [*Offering stuffed animal to MOM, who takes it*] Oh, I think Valerie should find a name for him.

MOM: And she will, too. Valerie has a gift for names. [*Cuddling the toy a bit*] Aren't we silly?

DAD: No, I think we're just risk-takers. [*Speaking to stuffed animal*] Do you want to try out this world? There are no guarantees, you know.

MOM: It can really knock the stuffings out of you! [*Responding in surprise to her own small joke*]

REALITY MAN: [*Again to BIBLE LADY*] I am still being realistic. In fact, more realistic than ever. Does a story end when we close the book? Not if the story has become part of us. So how could a play like this end with a few actors feeding each other lines, entering stage right, exiting stage left?

BIBLE LADY: The audience—

REALITY MAN: Of course. . . .

MOM and DAD approach the bed. MOM bends over, places the stuffed animal on the pillow, alongside the still averted head. THAN removes his hat and also strolls over toward the bed where he joins this little group.

DR. STERN: I myself slept with a teddy bear. Sometimes that teddy bear was the only creature in the house who had a hug all day long, and especially at night.

BIBLE LADY: I trust audiences. I really do. But is this play safe with them?

DR. STERN: And sometimes I think that is why I grew up with such a strong immune system. By hugging the teddy. He must have developed a terrific immune system, too.

REALITY MAN: We'll just have to trust them with it.

BIBLE LADY: Excuse me, this is where I get angry. [*She gets angry*] You don't expect me to buy that, do you! Where have you been? This is the TV generation—everything must be worked out between the last two commercial breaks! People expect it!

REALITY MAN: I don't know about that, some people—

BIBLE LADY: Stop talking while I'm interrupting! Will Valerie get
                her own name back and be able to fit into it? Who's
                going to answer that question, if we don't!
REALITY MAN: You're just working yourself up, ma'am—
BIBLE LADY: Not to mention is she going to recover or what—hah?
                Maybe she's gone already [*They both glance toward
                bed; the blue spot rises on bed: finds and settles focus
                on the two heads on the pillow.*]
DR. STERN: Anger is not unusual at these times. Some say it is
                healthy.
BIBLE LADY: Not to mention the raindrop. What's the significance of
                the raindrop—hah? Shouldn't we lay that out for them?

*MOM, DAD, THAN join hands. The blue light expands to include all of
them. Again, BIBLE LADY and REALITY MAN glance at that scene,
wonder, then return to their own.*

REALITY MAN: The reality is: each person is his own, her own reality.
                All must continue this story in their own way.
BIBLE LADY: Not to mention the moral. What are we supposed to
                learn from this—hah? Aren't we *supposed* to learn
                from this? Isn't dying OK and death and grief if we
                learn something from it? That's the buzz, brother.
                Buzz, buzz!

*REALITY MAN withdraws from BIBLE LADY and approaches bedside
group. Asks and receives permission to join them. The blue light
expands again. BIBLE LADY observes, and her mood transitions to
reflection/acceptance.*

*Music begins [Nielsen: The Fog is Lifting]. BIBLE LADY is trying to
decide about joining the others. When she speaks, it is as a barely over-
heard whisper. There are pauses, during where we hear the music without
interference*

BIBLE LADY: I don't have to go there. Not yet. I have good reasons
                not to . . . Books full of good reasons, and plenty more
                where they came from . . . I mean: just look at them!
                They've all let themselves get trapped . . . [*Confessing*

to the audience with her eyes] Oh . . . . . . right!
*[She joins the others by the bed. The blue light expands
again; she moves in a little closer to make sure she's
included]*

*As music ends, VALERIE enters, unseen by the bedside group that is facing
the other direction, hands joined. She carries what appears to be the same
stuffed animal that was placed on her pillow. Observes them a moment.
They do not seem to hear or respond as she speaks to or about them.*

VALERIE: *[To REALITY MAN]* I enjoyed the bike ride. I really
did. And the dance. And everything. *[To BIBLE LADY]*
That's such a lovely book when it's not being funny or
scary. I'd like us to read it together some day. *[To
THAN]* You, too: you're so much more important than
you can imagine! Mom! Dad! I haven't really been
away! And I know you've always been there! *[She all
but touches them caressingly, then takes a step forward
toward audience and, after a sign, speaks to audience]*

I sure made up a lot of stuff—I told you I would—Hope
I didn't make you mad. But now I have to go back.
[Glance toward bed] And you have places to go, too. It
was nice meeting you in this no place! *[Starts to turn
away, then halfturns back]* Remember—if you find
yourself in no place again—and no one is with you—
well—invite us over! *[Hugging stuffed animal]*

She runs off the stage as SNUFFY BARKS

Blackout

NOTEBOOK

At any age, life threatening illness also threatens to isolate a person from others. The painful sense of being abandoned and rejected can test the personal resources of the most mature and experienced individual. Anxiety, sorrow, and confusion may assail even the very old person who has lived well the proverbial "good life" and is at peace with self and God. There is still the need for human companionship and touch.

The Girl in the Raindrop faces an even more formidable situation. She has not yet had the time fully to become herself. She has not yet had career, husband, or children of her own. She has not yet had the opportunity to test wishes and beliefs against reality to shape her own definitive philosophy of life. And "never to be" could be the fate of all the adventures and fulfillments that a bright 13 year-old is capable of imagining.

Like an enfeebled resident in a skilled nursing home, Valerie is limited to a small compass of personal (well, actually rather impersonal) space. Similarly, her life is pretty much under the control of others. The routines are even more invasive and restrictive because she is receiving the best available aggressive treatment for her life-threatening disorder. She is also the subject of intellectual curiosity because Valerie's condition has proven resistant to the probings of the medico-scientific mind. The woman in the nursing home is much less interesting to the medical and scientific community because her "condition" is only old age and because there is little impulse to invest in treatment.

Part of Valerie's isolation can be understood as an unfortunate concomitant of the treatment protocol: she must be protected from infectious agents that could be inadvertently transmitted through human contact. Her most profound sense of isolation, however, comes from the loss of her closest supporting relationships: even when these desperately necessary people are with her, they're not really with her and, of course, she knows. The fact that it is their emotional pain, not indifference, that separates them does not relieve the distress.

Valerie, then, must somehow work out her destiny alone. How can she even approach the questions of meaning and value when she has not had the opportunity to discover her own self? And how can she persuade her elders—the all-knowing, all-powerful adults—to provide the key to understanding and comfort? The adult world and all its institutions are on trial here as one lonely and frightened girl turns to all conceivable resources.

Unlike some of the other theater pieces in this collection, *The Girl in the*

THE GIRL IN THE RAINDROP / 163

Raindrop really asks for an all-out production. Adequate rehearsal is vital. The cast must be given the opportunity to feel themselves into their roles. An ensemble spirit should be developed from the first moments of first readings. Physical actions must evolve naturally from character. Scene changes and effects must go like blazes. There is plenty of room, nevertheless, for artistic judgment and creative touches by director and cast. Bikeman can do his virtuoso tricks on an "air bike," for example, if he has the skill to bring this off. An imaginative yet disciplined choreographic sense is required to actualize Labyrinth I and II. Playfulness is just what we need at certain points, but the serious quest and the sudden moments of toppling into the void, or nearly so, must always ring true. Stage business for its own sake has no place here, as in any other drama.

Valerie is appealing, but too insightful and purposeful to ever be "cutesy." When well played, Bible Lady is also a sympathetic person who feels some strain in her commitment to being the source of constant reassurance. Bikeman also appears as Bird-Thanatric and Thanatric III. If Big Guy's delivery reminds the audience of Ronald Reagan about to board the presidential helicopter, so much the better.

Trust the audience to grasp and follow the emotional rhythms. And don't, please, "explain" this play to death in any postperformance discussion; use it instead to elicit the Valerie in all of us.

Woof!

You're right, Snuffy! I was getting too preachy. . . .

III. EPILOGUE

Arnie's Junkyard—*Or* How To Get Aging Out of the Trenches and Gerontologists Down from the Clouds

The agony of trench warfare made a profound impression on all who lived to tell (or refuse to tell) the tale. Although it was impossible to compensate for the suffering and loss, society could at least create a frame within which to memorialize this tragedy. It became known as "The Great War," or "The War to End All Wars." Finally the guns kept their silence and rows of white crosses symbolized death's harvest on the killing grounds. It seemed for a moment as though the days of horror had passed and could be safely encapsulated in the history books.

In retrospect, we know that a lethal epidemic of influenza soon took its toll, economic crises encouraged the development of militant tyrannies, and merciless conflicts continued to rage sporadically throughout a destabilized world. Even so, a new kind of happy hour made its debut in the United States. The postwar innovation of entertainment radio was followed by talkies on the silver screen, a golden age in sports, flappers, hip flasks, and all that jazz setting bodies in motion, not to mention an increasingly popular accouterment to a sexy and sophisticated lifestyle: the machine-rolled cigarette. True, life remained very difficult for the millions of Americans who were struggling to make it through The Great Depression. Nevertheless, there was diversion and fantasy aplenty. More significantly: The American Dream in which success crowns virtue and good works was still an article of faith. The older generation included many hardy men and women who had left the "old country" for the proverbial better life in America. Their belief, determination, and work ethos helped to sustain them through the hard times and to impel the younger generation forward. "The children will have what we didn't have" was both an agenda and a consolation.

ARNIE'S JUNKYARD

Decades later, a double-amputee veteran would tell me, "It was awful. Plain awful. The food, the mud, the rain, the trenches, the fleas, the lice, the rats. Day after day, no escape from it. And when the weather picked up a little, they'd send you right out to get yourself killed. Half Company D didn't even make it past the line (of barbed wire)."

Arnie was brooding more than usual at the moment because school children had visited his institutional residence, carrying tiny American flags and bearing small gifts. "What the hell do I do with a comb? They should have brought hair!" Arnie seldom discussed the military experience that had been such a crucial part of his life. "I did feel proud. For a long time. We had done that dirty job. Done it good. But what do we have to show for it now? You tell me!"

In Arnie's opinion, The War to End All Wars turned out not to have accomplished much, and he himself was now mired in a new kind of trench warfare that seemed no less hopeless and meaningless. "They mean well here," he conceded (as one of The They, I appreciated this acknowledgment). "But we all know what this place is. A junkyard for old wrecks! Hell, we're across the road from the town dump! Tell me that doesn't say something! So that's my life story, since you're interested. Write it down. Call it, *Arnie's Story: From the Stinking Trenches to the Stinking Junkyard*." Arnie actually didn't go on to tell all his story, to our loss. Here, as an inadequate substitute, is one gerontologist's story about his story. At the same time, it is a story about gerontologists, their gerontology, and the spirit of drama.

WHO'S THAT KNOCKING ON MY DOOR?

Arnie has a lot of company. The suspicion that doing one's best availeth nought became more prevalent after The War After The War to End All Wars. This new conflagration itself was quickly designated "World War II." Global destruction had lost its unique status as well as its claim to a justifying purpose. We just gave it a number.

Several unsettling, yet invigorating trends developed during the Post World War II (or, as many feared, pre-World War III) years. A disturbing new figure stalked across the European mind and soon knocked on the doors of an America that had been spared bloodshed on its own streets. "I am Existentialism. This is your wake-up call." (Norman Rockwell would not add this face to his portrait gallery.) Suicide was one of its calling cards: oh, the absurdity of life and, oh, the absurdity of death! So what did we do? As competents flourishing within The Land of Pragmatism, we rolled up our sleeves, started crisis centers, and established an American Association of Suicidology. Self-destruction became one more vexing problem we should try to do something about, like removing those stubborn stains from the carpet. ("I've tried everything, and the blood keeps coming back.") If Existentialism looked a bit disappointed at our inclination to take action instead of luxuriating in bleak introspection, well, tough for Existentialism!

At about the same time we were also confronted by other messengers of a world whose collective pants—I mean, defenses—had fallen down once too often. The larger issue of our relationship to mortality started to loom monstrously over the discomforting but relatively circumscribed problem of suicide. Perhaps it had been a mistake to answer that first rapping at the door. Let suicide in and the next thing you know, we discover that the rumor had something to it after all: *everybody* has a date with death. We were apprehensive, just like most people who are faced with the prospect of a blind date.

But, again, our capacity for innocent resilience came to the rescue. We convulsed at British-made parodies of our own funeral industry (Mitford, 1963; Waugh, 1977), and later imported British-made hospice programs with remarkable alacrity and effectiveness. As one of our own innovations, we reduced the chill of death anxiety to a 15-item true/false scale; as another, we added "death education" to "sex education" despite the protests of Good People Everywhere. Jake LaMotta would have been proud of us: we could "still roll with the punches."

One morning, however, a few of us noticed that Aurora, Goddess of Dawn, now was adorned with age spots and featured silvery threads among her tresses of gold. This awakening to a gray dawn did make us pause. We started to wonder: "Where are all these old people coming from?" And then: "Where are they all going—and who's paying their fare?" As the years have gone by, "We" have been turning into "They" and both the philosophical and the pragmatic questions have yet to be answered satisfactorily.

We did set to work as usual. An invitation to private soul-searching seems to stimulate our talent for establishing a busy, busy, busy set of task forces. We created committees, entitlements, research centers, and fetal-tissue-enhanced-youth-mimicking cosmetics. However, the age-related concerns have not gone away. The blessings of a long life have sometimes been difficult to discern when one has out-lived intimate companions and financial resources.

Meanwhile, opinion leaders have taken up the task of again updating the image of elderly people. Arnie's age-mates, for example, were entering the ranks of the used up and useless as they reached their sixties soon after the end of World War II. (Arnie himself had already become accustomed to his own more distinctive role as a person who made others uncomfortable with his visible losses—aging actually did something to soften this impact on society's tender sensitivities.)

A few years later, gerontology had set up shop. Concurrently, sentiment and conscience flowed toward this newly discovered wound. Aged people were now more likely to be conceived as victims and casualties. It was not just Arnie: all elders were veterans of life's harsh ordeals, and therefore deserved compassion and assistance. The tune played upon collective feelings of guilt was counterpointed by the realization that we all would have to dance to it some day. Furthermore, unlike mortality with its mysteries and lovely ambiguities, aging was all too palpable. Here and there a face could be lifted, a tummy tucked, or a rear end realigned. Nevertheless, aging earned grudging respect as a relentless enemy. As we started to reach out to frail and needy elders we were at the same time feeling more than a little sorry for ourselves and nervous about our own fates.

A subtle play of lights and shadows soon introduced a variation on this theme. Elders became role models brimming over with wisdom and traditional values. This attitude shift could be seen within gerontology as well as those media mavens who recognized society's hunger for wisdom and traditional values, or—preferably—a simplistic facsimile. Characterful old visages could glare formidably from the television screen and sell us plain, honest, nonfancy-doodled cereal or cadge us into making financial investments. ("We make money the old fashioned way: by risking yours!")

Furthermore, wisdom did not stand in the way of golf, travel, romance, and other emblems of the good life. For the providential and fortunate, "retirement" (a term by now well hated) provided a second chance at adolescence—this time with the experience, judgment, and confidence to actually enjoy it. In these and other ways, society made an effort to see aging in a positive light. And, indeed, the lives of some elderly men and women provided encouraging affirmation this possibility. Arnie, however, did not have his share of this windfall. By the time society's image-making apparatus had reconstructed aged people as wise and valuable, Arnie had become aphasic as the result of a stroke. Furthermore his indescribable glare of pained defiance did not attract those seeking warm and fuzzy interactions with an idealized old man.

The opinion factory concurrently is experimenting with still another new product. Although offered as an innovation, the image of the elder as a selfish and parasitic organism borrows much from the resentment that has often been engendered by gerontocracy. In traditional societies, power has often been wielded by the elders (Keith, 1985). The breakaway colonies that became the United States showed less than the customary respect for vested authority. The new political system and socio-cultural climate encouraged independence, daring, and self-interest. The old world was both shocked and thrilled by our adventurism and our inclination to thumb our nose at authority, privilege, and gerontocracy.

And so, the opinion leaders are again busy, busy, busy. Too many people are getting too old. It's one thing to have a few sages and saints on hand (Kastenbaum, 1990; in press), but quite another to deal with a large population of long-lived people who hold strong opinions and are not willing to dance for pennies. Elders who were cast as victims not that long ago have now become villains who are overtaxing our health care system when ill and having it rather too pleasant when they're not.

For "senior citizens" who want to keep their images up to date, these last decades have been more than a little confusing! It is not just that social constructions of old age (and childhood . . . and adolescence . . .) have been changing. Redefinitions of age-related attributes and values are part of a continuing historical process (Cole, 1989; Troyansky, 1992). It is the rapid turnover and sharp-edge differences in images that attests to our insecurity with the meaning of aging and the value of the elderly person. "Who am I supposed to be this morning?"

Replacing one image of the elderly person with another has not quite done it. The same may be said for activism and meliorism. "Doing something about old age" has not quite done it. Both society at large and gerontology at small have made real advances in recent decades. Nevertheless, we have neither mastered the societal challenges nor quelled the private anxieties. Perhaps—just perhaps—this time we might actually have to *think* about the human condition. We might actually have to come to terms with our most cherished assumptions, fervent hopes, and anxiety-closet nightmares. (Unless, of course, we are willing to commission Dr. Death to think for us.)

BEST AND WORST CASE SCENARIOS

A distinguished therapist observes that "I meet my clients when they are lost in their dark wood. Words such as 'It doesn't make sense,' 'I feel like I am in limbo,' 'I have an empty feeling within me,' are signals that what made sense before, what held life together, what patterns of significance and intentionality, has broken apart thrusting these individuals into a transitional stage between the new and the old. This can be very frightening: after all, even though the old way is not working, at least it was known" (Carlsen, 1988, p. 3). What Mary Baird Carlsen has discovered on the individual level is also symptomatic of society at large. There is a pervasive suspicion that "It" does not make sense, that we are all in limbo, and that even the most fortunate and successful suffer from "that empty feeling."

The worst case scenario is no longer the prospect of failure, loss, or frustrated desire. Negative outcomes are known to be "part of the game," intrinsic to the risks and vulnerabilities of life. Arnie, for example, reconciled himself both to the combat injury that reduced his options in life and to the ailments and limitations that accompanied his aging process. As he might have said—"Hell's bells! War is dangerous. Any fool knows that! And if you're going to keep slogging along through life, of course you're going to look and feel your age!" What kept eating away at Arnie was the feeling that his life just plain didn't matter to anybody.

Some years later I would come to know many people whose "sunset years" actually were being spent in the sun (Kastenbaum, 1993). They lived in attractive homes in planned adult-only communities and enjoyed such amenities as golf courses and swimming pools. With respect to health, finances, climate, and companionship they were a good deal more fortunate than Arnie. Nevertheless, it was also common for these people to feel troubled and oppressed. They did live rather well in their little island fortresses: but on every side they were surrounded by the ignorant, the misguided, the disrespectful. Even—or especially—governmental agencies did not respect and uphold traditional values. Objectively, there was much to relish in their lives; subjectively, however, they often felt that their values had been forgotten or rejected by society at large. Whether in the dark woods of a state geriatric facility or the morning sunshine of their own homes, the questions kept repeating themselves: "So what's the point?" "Does it all add up to anything?" "Have I had a life?"

Similarly, the best case scenario does not necessarily require posting a high score in the game of life. Individuals who judge that they have conducted themselves in accordance with personal and social values are likely to feel content even if some of the big prizes have eluded them. "We did the right thing!" and "I gave it all that I had" are illustrative verdicts. This kind of self-assessment can still be heard from people who put aside their own personal hopes in order to protect the survival of their families during the Great Depression. Many years later they do not have the college degree, the professional career or other palpable trophy that had once motivated them. However, they have earned their own self-acceptance by "playing the cards life gave me" in accordance with their family and societal values. A parallel phenomenon can be seen among artists, writers, composers, and others who pursue creative goals. More often than not, their works are ignored or rejected for extended periods of time. In following their own inner promptings and visions they may be "out of fashion" through much of their careers. Nevertheless, the intrinsic satisfaction of creating according to their own values often has triumphed over the elusive rewards of acclaim and prosperity.

In discussing their life work with interviewer Connie Goldman (1986), elderly artists repeatedly emphasized the sense of fulfillment that they discover in the process of creation. They also expressed concern for the younger generation who are faced with a situation in which "Anything is as good as anything else; there are no rules to break and no peaks to climb. You can't fail, and so you can't really achieve anything either, unless you have established your own standards."

Whether one captures or misses out on the prizes of life is not a matter of indifference. Some elders still fester in bitterness and frustration over that promotion or other opportunity that was denied them long ago.

Nevertheless, experiences teaches that best and worse case scenarios have more to do with one's sense of active allegiance to a guiding principle than to palpable and public outcomes. Active allegiance to a guiding principle ensures a degree of satisfaction, self-acceptance, and integrity. Again, Arnie: "We had done that dirty job. Done it good." It is finding oneself bereft of a dependable guiding principle that contributes most to the worst case scenario. "Hollow victory" and "empty success" are not oxymorons. Such terms well describe the sense of profound disappointment—often accompanied by alienation and doubt—when one has achieved something held to be important only to find that it really doesn't seem to matter very much after all.

Arnie's solo, "But what do we have to show for it now?" is actually part of a fragmented choral lamentation that is heard from elderly voices throughout the land. The principles that guided their lives no longer seem to be respected and cherished. Residents of senior adult communities may cultivate a protective strategy that may be likened to the keepers of a fortress under siege. Their encrustation (Kastenbaum, 1993) serves not only to ward off enemies (abhorrent government policies, people of different racial and ethnic composition, etc.), but also to cover up the wound of insult and deprecation.

To put it another way: the story is not turning out as one might have expected. The men and women who have lived through much of the twentieth century could shape their expectations around rules and values of a modernizing world that still drew upon the images and rhetoric of earlier times. To be sure, there were tensions between the aggressive and individualistic spirit of American-style modernization and the ties that bound one to home, church, conformity, and obedience. However, it is the accelerating pattern of change since midcentury that has opened the major rift within and between people.

Most relevantly, the postmodernizing world has called into question the assumption that one's life is a story that can be coherently lived and told. We hear this discord plainly in the angular, fragmented, grinding, and nonsequential music created by experimentalists working within classical, jazz, or rock traditions. And we hear its mirror image in numbing, repetitive, tranquilizing, low-event New Age music. Another cardinal feature of contemporary music (including some of the most masterful) is its looting of the past for points of references and relief. The "art" music of today frequently devotes itself to commenting on the music of other times. Even when inventive, humorous or poignant, this music seems unable to find its own voice and tell its own story.

The visual arts have been even more effective in deconstructing our habits and frames of perception. Within a relatively short time, images originating with Dali, Magritte, Ernst, Picasso, Warhol and other once-alarming modernists have entered into the cultural repertoire. Television commercials and music videos, for example, offer many a variation on surrealistic, dada, and superrealistic themes. The postmodern gallery of visual images offers brusque disjunctions and displacements, often behaving as though in accordance with dream logic. We are often a long way removed from "pretty pictures that tell a sensible story." Neither the museum nor the concert hall provide security for the troubled person who is attempting to affirm linearity, continuity, motivation, and coherence amidst subtle loss and turbulent change. It is through no coincidence that the American Association of Suicidology adopted as its icon Edvard Munch's *The Scream,* a harrowing image of a person melting into anxiety while attempting to cross a bridge.

A visit to the theater could also prove hazardous to what is left of one's mental health. The most creative and disturbing innovation of the postwar years was the "theater of the absurd," which lived up to its billing as characters searched for authors, transformed themselves into rhino's, or waited for Godot. It was not just what was happening on stage that was so preposterous and vexing. The real nasty business transpired as the implicit relationship between theater and reality, between character and player, and between player and audience was shaken to its foundation (six nights a week, with a matinee on Saturday).

Perhaps one should stay home, then, and read a good book. But one must hope that the book is not by Derrida (1978) or his kith and kin. In postmodernistic hands, the innocent, time-honored relationship between reader and text (and author) dissolves into a surrealistic infinite regress. Perhaps one can no longer even speak of "a text," but must instead defer to an indeterminate process of "texting." We might as well blame Heisenberg as well while we're at it—his notorious principle of uncertainty has swaggered away from its origins in subatomic physics and now strides freely through the entire range of science, scholarship, and art.

Certainty appears elusive if not illusionary. Continuity and coherence are problematical. One need only catch the news on radio or television. Each brief item is isolated from those preceding and following. Sequence is their only commonality, and the results of last night's basketball game may be conveyed with stronger feeling than the passing mention of a natural disaster that killed hundreds in another part of the world. What the "informed" listener or viewer really learns is that one thing is about the same as another and that there is no connection or coherence to be sought or discovered. News item replaces news item, just as year replaces year, and person replaces person. The most bizarre music video with its flashy costumes and effects is less discombobulating than the routine newscast with its bland, empty, and decontextualized recital.

Erikson (1979), Butler (1963) and subsequent advocates of a life review in the later adult years have mostly emphasized the intrapsychic processes involved. Now we must also take very seriously the transitional socio-symbolic context within which these processes operate. By which set of rules and expectations are elderly individuals to place their lives in perspective? Should self-judgment rest on a foundation of assumptions and beliefs that are no longer shared by society at large? Or should an aged person attempt to "go with the flow" of a superaccelerated, high-tech, relativistic, and consumption-oriented society? Is it desirable—or even possible—to construct a self-narrative that encompasses perhaps eight or nine decades of unprecedented change? Munch's angst-ridden creature is still screaming on the bridge; characters are still searching for their author. Coming to terms with one's entire self across the life course has always been a challenge; doing so when this life course has been co-extensive with the brilliant, terrifying, and absurdist twentieth century may pose the greatest such challenge ever encountered.

DOING GERONTOLOGY BY THE NUMBERS

Not only aging but the study of aging must find its way in a changing world. As Einstein observed (was it in the elevator or the train?), it is not "pure" velocity but relative motion that can really drive us bonkers. There would be much less stress, fragmentation and alienation if everything and everybody were accelerating at the same tempo. A reasonably sober and attentive orchestra can turn on its *accelerando* as deftly as a racing car driver while preserving pitch, tone, harmony, and cohesion. The difficulty—for gerontology as well as its subject-matter—is to be found in the premature, ragged, and delinquent "entrances" into postmodern tempo.

Personality, generational, gender, ethnic-cultural, occupational, and institutional differences can be discerned in response to the emerging opportunities and challenges to traditional values. Some of us are leaping ahead, some staying behind. Apart from whatever may be the intrinsic merits and foibles of both approaches, it is this pulling-apartness that places additional strain on social cohesiveness. (It's not easy to offer a neighborly "Howdy" as one strolls down the street and encounters—briefly—a streaking rollerblade operative who is quivering to headphoned music. Are both really on the same street?)

Gerontology's response has been influenced by its place in the history of science as well as by the overall forces of technological progress and social change. The systematic study of aging and the aged showed up late—but perhaps not late enough—in the procession of newly differentiating scientific disciplines. Being a recent arrival means that gerontology does not have deep sustaining traditions and matured perspectives. In effect, those who study oldness are themselves among the newest kids on the block. This lack of firm disciplinary tradition has its advantages. We should be—or could be—more footloose and adventurous, although this proposition is difficult to affirm when one examines mainstream paradigms, procedures, and concepts. The prime disadvantage is that gerontology does not have its own distinctive viewpoint or creed to draw upon as an alternative to the general fads and flux of scientific fashion.

Paradoxically, gerontology may also have emerged too soon. Had we bided our time a little longer we might have entered in a more innovative and sophisticated frame of mind. There is a genre of jesting which features the line, "That doesn't take a rocket scientist" (alternatively: ". . . brain surgeon"). Well, there is something to these comparisons. Theoretical physicists and the best minds concerning themselves with the brain have developed paradigms and concepts that leave Dr. Geront eating the dust of nineteenth century contrivances. Sociobehavioral and not a little of biogerontology still rely upon paradigms that have outlived their usefulness, paradigms from the industrial era in which one can still hear the gears laboriously grinding, the levers creaking, the cranks cranking, and the steam whistling. Prevalent methods and explanations remain doggedly mechanistic. Simplistic push or pull theories and cause-effect chains continue to make for heavy going. The revolution/evolution of scientific/philosophic thought since the Einsteins made their point has made little impact in our field. Dr. Geront has become respectable by carrying forward many of industrial science's founding assumptions, concepts, and methods, but Dr. Geront might not recognize a late twentieth century theory if it walked up and bit him/her. Although some elders are coping resourcefully with postmodernity, the gerontological establishment, in general, is still puttering with its antique equipment and operation manual. Here, then, is a most relevant example of relative motion: gerontology choosing or allowing itself to follow the old dusty road rather than dare a bolder conceptual and methodological approach.

"Doing gerontology by the numbers" refers to more than our tendency to design studies with cookie-cutters in hand. It has to do with the relationships among number, thought, and situated action. In brief:

- "Number" is an astounding and mysterious concept. One can readily forgive some appreciative souls for worshiping number or attempting to explain the inexplicable through numerology. If the concept of number were first discovered or invented this morning, it would be more electrifying than electricity. Casual familiarity has dulled our appreciation for this strangely beautiful and beautifully strange companion to the human epic.
- Mathematical principles and formulae can be the glorious offspring of number. Number become principle can lead to remarkable predictions, discoveries, and innovations. We may first catch sight of some truths through recognition of mathematical relationships, and then struggle later to generate a complementary verbal/semantic model.
- Statistics do not operate at the same exalted level. Useful as they can be, statistics have little talent for discovering or constructing reality. A mathematical principle or formula that is eventually found to be flawed may nevertheless sharpen our abilities to read the heavens. A flawless statistical analysis, on the other hand, may teach us nothing about ourselves or the world in which we live. Mathematical thinking can provide guidance; statistical analyses require guidance by resourceful and disciplined thought.
- Gerontology has produced its share of useful statistics. These figures do not automatically add up to anything, however. Most of our statistics have been generated by studies that are essentially atheoretical. At their best, the statistics provide a useful kind of summary-description from a potentially richer data set. Statistics also provide the raw (actually, the cooked or half-baked) material for making judgements regarding differences and correlations. But no matter how high grows the mound of computer print-out, no striking new theory, no overarching principle, no radically innovative model will emerge. The abandoned lover mourns that only "When cockle shells become silver bells will my love return to me." The cockle shells of statistics will never become the silver bells of understanding.

Consider, if you will, one example of our current uneasy relationships among number, thought, and situated action. Some of the most sophisticated research strategies known to adult development and aging are those that go by such names as time-lag or cross-sequential. These are prospective or real-time studies that attempt to integrate the best features of cross-sectional and longitudinal designs. Baltes (1968) and Schaie (1984) were the pioneers in formulating and advocating this exemplary approach.

So what's the problem? Both cross-sectional and longitudinal designs utilize real people: either different people of different ages at the same time of measurement, or the same people growing older at repeated points of measurement. Although each of these basic designs has its limits and flaws, each rests securely on its real-person base. The more complex and ambitious time-lag design also begins with real people at Time 1, and adds another wave of real people at Time 2. There may be further waves of new participants as the study continues, and all participants, of course, continue to age as they move through their lives in real time.

The funny stuff begins after the data are harvested. Not surprisingly, these data are in coded and quantitative form. Perhaps we should remind ourselves that even at this early point, the researcher's data looks, feels, and acts not at all like the people from whom they were harvested. What happens next is a series of rather sophisticated statistical analyses that further extends the separation of statistics from people. The statistical legerdemain is admirable on its own terms and provides valuable instructional material for budding researchers. The more advanced the analysis, however, the less is the resemblance between the statistics and the people or, to put it another way, the less tangible is their ontological relationship.

Remember "real people?" Long gone! The end product statistics represent the differences between differences between people. Depending upon the particular research design and the particular choice of statistical package, we may even be dealing with the differences between the differences of the differences between differences. Or better! (or worse!). Time-lag designs have the laudable purpose of differentiating between several sets of possible influence, such as age, time of measurement, and elapsed (real) time. To compare and evaluate these sources of influences, the statistical treatment violates the integrity of the Real Actual Person (RAP).

The RAP can be only in one place, behaving in one way, at any particular time. By contrast the Statistically Invented Person (SIP) hovers like a disenfranchised spirit. The SIP in a time-lag study is a more evolved progeny of the famous 2.3 children and 1.6 automobiles that surveyors have often cataloged as part of the American home. Just as there really are no 2.3 children (RAP), so the end product statistics from a time-lag study yield higher order composite portraits that do not describe the behavior of any one individual at any one point in time. In fact, it is only a certain faltering or inconsistency in the conventions of statistical analysis that avoids such conclusions as: "Femininity increases as a function of cohort, time of measurement, and chronological age." Samples as a whole do shift toward the female side of the gender distribution as they move through time. We happen to know that this trend is the result of God's desire to gather men to his bosom earlier. But the statistics don't know this, and the statisticians won't let the statistics show themselves to be so transparently ludicrous. Yet the SIPs do slip past us and, once past the laboratory door, they are free to infiltrate textbooks, lectures, background papers for congressional hearings, etc. There is just no traceable and usable relationship between the end product statistics from most of these sophisticated studies and RAP attempting to cope with their lives.

Trenchant researchers such as Baltes and Schaie themselves are aware that their statistical products cannot be applied directly to real people in real life situations. They have on occasion issued appropriate cautions to others and have themselves generally limited the utilization of these statistical findings to the examination of broad theoretical issues (e.g., the trajectory of intelligence across the life course). Others, however, are understandably tempted to draw real life conclusions from these careful and elaborate studies.

SIPs can be valuable for theoretical purposes that are several steps removed from real life situations. However, we would be naive to expect these phantoms of the computer to provide us with new paradigms or images of the developing and aging person. The statistical outcomes do not approach the grandeur and purity of mathematical principles, nor are they guided by creative envisionings. Even the most expensive cockle shells will never become silver bells.

DEFINING ACTS

Gerontology has not yet succeeded in providing a comprehensive, coherent, and theoretically invigorating account of its subject matter. Arnie, his brethren in sunbelt retirement communities, and elders throughout the nation are confronted with their own challenge of constructing meaningful life narratives within the unsettled and unsettling context of postmodern society. So here is a suggestion.

Let us add another arena in which both the self-comprehending and gerontological enterprise might advance and flourish. This is the arena of dramatic encounter, interaction, conflict, and transformation. It provides a natural testing grounds for thoughts, doubts, fears, yearnings, and intuitions that tend to be denied expression in the scrimmage of everyday life as well as in the projects of researchers and policy-makers. Aging *is* drama. All we need do, basically, is to provide the frame and opportunity for this drama to emerge in ways that will be instructive to the participants themselves and to gerontology.

This approach has been prefigured by several perceptive observers, including Berman's (1988) study of diaries and journals, Erikson's (1979) examination of Dr. Borg's life as distilled in the Bergman film, *Wild Strawberries,* Chinen's (1989; 1992) elucidation of folk tales, and Kaminsky's storytelling about story telling (1993). Furthermore, there has existed for some time now a theory that connects the language of dramatic action with social and behavioral sciences as well as the humanities. *A Grammar of Motives* (Burke, 1962) offers dramatism as an approach to understanding the complexity of human experience in "real life" as well as in the theater and literature. Burke uses five terms "as generating principle of our investigation. They are: Act, Scene, Agent, Agency, Purpose . . . any complete statement about motives will offer some kind of answer to these five questions: what was done (act), when or where it was done (scene), who did it (agent), how he did it (agency), and why (purpose)" (op. cit., p. xv). Burke's ideas have been influential in performance studies, literary criticism, and related areas. His broad-ranging style of presentation may be problematic for readers who prefer a tight focus and "cutting to the chase." I am not so sure that the specifics of his theory would meet the needs and interests of social gerontologists, but Burke has demonstrated, if any demonstration was necessary, that the dramatist paradigm is well suited to the challenge of understanding the complexities of human thought, feeling, and action.

One must now add the idea of "dramatic truth." A drama can fail in script or performance when something about it fails to ring true. Players and audience recognize at once the false note that creeps into a characterization or the contrived turn of plot. The simplest gesture or intonation can betray a failure of authenticity. Such failures are more immediate and palpable than the results of most statistical tests or rational analyses. What constitutes dramatic truth will vary from play to play, even from scene to scene. But truth will out—or do us in, whether in a knockabout farce or a tragedy.

Acknowledging aging as drama can restore the primacy of situated action. Charts, figures, statistical tables and words on paper have constructed their own replacement reality that perpetuates itself rather apart from the living experience of RAPs. Even the script for a play lies dormant until it is actualized through performance. Situated action whether on or off stage brings the immediacy that identifies, tests, affirms, and, occasionally, transforms our being.

- Every significant theorem deserves testing through situated dramatic action as well as through quantitative analysis.
- The guiding conceptions of gerontology should make room for the questings, encounters, conflicts, and scenes that are at the heart of our lives.
- Existing concepts and methods on such topics as diary and journal writing, storytelling, expressive arts, role playing and psychodrama should be allied with the most compelling and incisive techniques used to create good theater.
- Caregivers, administrators, and policy-makers should develop their sensitivities to the dramatic realities of the lives they influence.
- Elderly men and women should have the opportunity to rediscover themselves not only through ruminative life reviews but also through defining acts. "So—this is who I am! This is what I have become! This is what I yet might be!"

At the moment, Arnie and his buddies are still in the trenches and gerontology is still pretty much in the cloudy, cloudy clouds. Arnie could use the perspective that might be offered by those fortunate enough to be yet among the quick. Gerontologists should be capable of appreciating the experiential perspective for its own truth, rather than merely for the fragmented data that can be skinned off. All of us will never be quite sure how our life stories go until we expose ourselves to definitional acts.

Bibliography

Baltes, P. B., Longitudinal and Cross-sectional Sequences in the Study of Age and Generation Effects, *Human Development, 11*, pp. 145-171, 1968.

Berman, H. J., Admissable Evidence: Geropsychology and the Personal Journal, in *Qualitative Gerontology,* S. Reinharz and G. D. Rowles (eds.), Springer, New York, pp. 47-63, 1988.

Burke, K., *A Grammar of Motives,* University of California, Berkeley, 1962.

Butler, R. N., The Life Review: An Interpretation of Reminiscence in Old Age, *Psychiatry, 26,* pp. 65-76, 1963.

Carlsen, M. B., *Meaning-Making. Therapeutic Processes in Adult Development,* W. W. Norton, New York, 1988.

Chinen, A. B., *In the Ever After,* Chiron, Wilmette, Illinois, 1989.

Chinen, A. B., *Once Upon a Midlife,* Tarcher, Los Angeles, 1992.

Cole, T. R., Generational Equity in America: A Cultural Historian's Perspective, *Social Science and Medicine, 29,* pp. 377-383, 1989.

Derrida, J., *Writing and Difference,* University of Chicago Press, Chicago, 1978.

Erikson, E. H., Reflections on Dr. Borg's Life Cycle, in *Aging, Death, and the Completion of Being,* D. D. Van Tassel (ed.), University of Pennsylvania Press, Philadelphia, pp. 29-68, 1979.

Goldman, C., *Elders of the Tribe,* Audio cassette, Connie Goldman Productions, Los Angeles, 1986.

Kaminsky, M., Story of the Shoe Box: On the Meaning and Practice of Transmitting Stories, in *Handbook of the Humanities and Aging,* T. R.

Cole, D. D. Van Tassel, and R. Kastenbaum (eds.), Springer, New York, pp. 307-328, 1993.

Kastenbaum, R., The Age of Saints and the Saintliness of Age, *International Journal of Aging and Human Development, 30,* pp. 95-118, 1990.

Kastenbaum, R., Encrusted Elders: Arizona and the Political Spirit of Postmodern Aging, in *Voices and Visions of Aging. Toward a Critical Gerontology,* T. R. Cole, W. A. Achenbaum, P. L. Jakobi, and R. Kastenbaum (eds.), Springer, New York, pp. 160-183, 1993.

Kastenbaum, R., The Sage, the Saint, and the SOB: Three Models of Successful Aging, *Journal of Geriatric Psychiatry,* in press.

Keith, J., Age in Anthropological Research, in *Handbook of Aging and the Social Sciences, Second Edition,* R. H. Binstock and Ethel Shanas (eds.), Van Nostrand Reinhold, New York, pp. 231-263, 1985.

Mitford, N., *The American Way of Death,* Simon & Schuster, New York, 1963.

Schaie, K. W., Historical Time and Cohort Effects, in *Life-span Developmental Psychology: Historical and Generational Effects,* K. A. McCluskey and H. W. Reese (eds.), Academic Press, New York, pp. 109-128, 1984.

Troyansky, D. G., The Older Person in the Western World: From the Middle Ages to the Industrial Revolution, in *Handbook of the Humanities and Aging,* T. R. Cole, D. D. Van Tassel, and R. Kastenbaum (eds.), Springer, New York, pp. 40-61, 1992.

Waugh, E., *The Loved One,* Chapman & Hall, London, 1977.